STILL MORE
HIGH SCHOOL
TALKSH...S

FOR AGES 14-18

D1373076

50 CREATIVE
DISCUSSIONS
FOR YOUR YOUTH GROUP

DAVID ROGERS

ZONDERVAN®

ZONDERVAN.com/
AUTHORTRACKER
follow your favorite authors

youth
specialties

YOUTH SPECIALTIES

Still More High School Talksheets: 50 Creative Discussions for Your Youth Group
Copyright 2009 by David Rogers

Youth Specialties resources, 300 S. Pierce St., El Cajon, CA 92020 are published by Zondervan, 5300 Patterson Ave. SE, Grand Rapids, MI 49530.

ISBN 978-0-310-28492-5

All Scripture quotations, unless otherwise indicated, are taken from the *Holy Bible, Today's New International Version*™. TNIV®. Copyright 2001, 2005 by International Bible Society. Used by permission of Zondervan. All rights reserved.

Any Internet addresses (websites, blogs, etc.) and telephone numbers printed in this book are offered as a resource. They are not intended in any way to be or imply an endorsement by Youth Specialties, nor does Youth Specialties vouch for the content of these sites and numbers for the life of this book.

All rights reserved. No part of this publication may be reproduced, stored in a retrieval system, or transmitted in any form or by any means — electronic, mechanical, photocopy, recording, or any other — except for brief quotations in printed reviews, without the prior permission of the publisher.

Cover design by David Conn
Interior design by Brandi Etheredge Design

Printed in the United States of America

09 10 11 12 13 14 • 20 19 18 17 16 15 14 13 12 11 10 9 8 7 6 5 4 3 2

I am humbled that God placed me in a family tree with such deep roots and sturdy branches. You all are life to me. I thank God for you and deeply love you. Alison, Jack and Lucy: Thank you for allowing me to put on paper whatGod has put in me during my years of following Jesus while also trying to lead our family well. Mom and Dad, Sarah, Andy, Kelli, Brody and Lane, Grandmother and Granddaddy Ford, Grandmother and Granddaddy Rogers, Ernie,Mary, Leslie, Natalie and Nate, John, Mary Ellen, Katherine and Johnny, Dick, Kay, Richard, Elizabeth and Robbie, Larry and Rita, Josh, April and Ryder. Thanks also to Bob, Neil, Louie, Busby, Lightsey, Mark, Bake, Dean, Jeremy, Gary, John, Richard, Eddie, Tommy, Chris, Robbie, Crowder, J.R., Greg, Jim, Rick and Bev, Bill and Connie, Bruce and Jan, Ron, Rhodes, Burns, Toop, and Mr. Hollis: Bless you for blessing me in life, friendship, and ministry.

CONTENTS

THE HOWS AND WHATS OF TALKSHEETS

Each of the 50 discussions includes a reproducible TalkSheet for your students to work on, as well as simple, step-by-step instructions on how to use it. All you need is this book, some Bibles, a few copies of the handouts, and some kids (some food won't hurt, either).

These TalkSheets are user-friendly and very flexible. They can be used in youth group meetings, Sunday school classes, or in Bible study groups. You can adapt them for either large or small groups. And they can be covered in only 20 minutes or explored more intensively. You can build an entire youth group meeting around a single TalkSheet, or you can use TalkSheets to supplement other materials and resources you might be covering.

LEADING A TALKSHEET DISCUSSION

TalkSheets can be used as a curriculum for your youth group, but they're designed as springboards for discussion. They encourage your kids to take part and interact with each other. And hopefully they'll do some serious thinking, discover new ideas, defend their points of view, and make decisions.

Youth today live in an active world that bombards them with the voices of society and the media—most of which drown out what they hear from the church. Youth leaders must teach the church's beliefs and values—and help young people make the right choices in a world full of options.

A TalkSheet discussion works for this very reason. While dealing with the questions and activities on the TalkSheet, your kids will think carefully about issues, compare their beliefs and values with others and with Scripture, and make their own choices. TalkSheets will challenge your group to explain and rework their ideas in a Christian atmosphere of acceptance, support, and growth.

Maybe you're asking yourself, *What will I do if the kids in my group just sit there and don't say anything?* Well, when kids don't have anything to say, a lot of times it's because they haven't had a chance or time to get their thoughts organized. Most young people haven't developed the ability to think on their feet. Since many are afraid they might sound stupid, they often avoid voicing their ideas and opinions.

The solution? TalkSheets let your kids deal with the issues in a challenging but non-threatening way before the actual discussion begins. They'll have time to organize their thoughts, write them down, and ease their fears about participating. They may even look forward to sharing their answers. Most importantly, they'll want to find out what others said and open up to talk through the topics.

If you're still a little leery about leading a discussion with your kids, that's okay—the only way to get them rolling is to get them started.

YOUR ROLE AS THE LEADER

The best discussions don't happen by accident. They require careful preparation and a sensitive, enthusiastic, and caring leader. Don't worry if you aren't experienced or don't have hours to prepare. TalkSheets are designed to help even the novice leader. The more TalkSheet discussions you lead, the easier it becomes. So keep the following tips in mind when using the TalkSheets as you get your kids talking:

BE CHOOSY

Choose a TalkSheet based on the needs and the maturity level of your group. Don't feel obligated to use the TalkSheets in the order they appear in this book. Use your best judgment and mix them up any way you want.

TRY IT YOURSELF

Once you've chosen a TalkSheet for your group, answer the questions and do the activities yourself. Though each Talksheet session has a similar structure, they each contain different activities. Imagine your kids' reactions to the TalkSheet. This will help you prepare for the discussion and understand what you're asking them to do. Plus, you'll have some time to think of other appropriate questions, activities, and Bible verses that help tailor it to your kids.

GET SOME INSIGHT

On each leader's guide page, you'll find numerous tips and ideas for getting the most out of your discussion. You may want to add some of your own thoughts or ideas in the margins. And there's room to keep track of the date and the name of your group at the top of the leader's page. You'll also find suggestions for additional activities and discussion questions.

There are some references to Internet links throughout the TalkSheets. These are guides for you to find the resources and information you need. For additional help, be sure to visit the Youth Specialties Web site at www.YouthSpecialties.com for information on materials and other links for finding what you need. Be careful as you use the Internet and videos—you'll need to (carefully!) preview them first (if applicable, you might need to check with your supervisor if you aren't sure if they're appropriate) and try to avoid any surprises.

MAKE COPIES

Your students will need their own copies of the TalkSheet—but make sure you only make copies of the student's side of the TalkSheet. The material on the reverse side (the leader's guide) is just for you. Remember: You're permitted to make copies for your group because we've said you can—but just for your youth group…not for every youth group in your state! U.S. copyright laws haven't changed, and it's still mandatory to request permission before making copies of published material. Thank you for cooperating.

INTRODUCE THE TOPIC

It's important to have a definite starting point to your session and introduce the topic before you pass out your TalkSheets to your group. Depending on your group, keep it short and to the point. Be careful to avoid over-introducing the topic, sounding preachy, or resolving the issue before you've started. Your goal is to spark your students' interest and leave plenty of room for discussion. You may also want to tell a story, share an experience, or describe a situation or problem having to do with the topic. You might want to jump-start your group by asking something like, "What's the first thing you think of when you hear the word _____ [insert the word here]?" After a few answers, you can add something like, "Well, it seems we all have different ideas about this subject. Tonight we're going to investigate it a bit further…"

The following are excellent methods you can use to introduce any lesson in this book—

• Show a related short film or video.
• Read a passage from a book or magazine that relates to the subject.
• Play a popular song that deals with the topic.
• Perform a short skit or dramatic presentation.

- Play a simulation game or role-play, setting up the topic.
- Present current statistics, survey results, or read a newspaper article that provides recent information about the topic.
- Use posters, videos, or other visuals to help focus attention on the topic.

THE OPENER

We've designed the OPENER to be a great kick-off to the discussion. Some may work better to use **before** you pass out the Talksheets. Others may work better as discussion starters **after** the students have completed their Talksheets. You decide! Check out the MORE section, too—it often contains an alternate opening idea or activity that'll help get students upbeat and talking, which is perfect for leading an effective TalkSheet discussion. TIP: When you're leading a game or OPENER, consider leading it like a game-show host would. Now that may not sound very spiritual, but if you think about what a host does (builds goodwill, creates excitement, facilitates community, listens to others) that sounds pretty pastoral, doesn't it? Plus, it makes it more fun!

ALLOW ENOUGH TIME

Pass out copies of the TalkSheet to your kids after the OPENER and make sure each person has a pen or pencil and a Bible. There are usually four to six discussion activities on each TalkSheet. If your time is limited, or if you're using only a part of the Talk-Sheet, tell the group to complete only the activities you'd like them to complete.

Decide ahead of time if you'd like your students to work on the TalkSheets individually or in groups. Sometimes the TalkSheet will already have students working in small groups. Let them know how much time they have for completing the TalkSheet, then

again when there's a minute (or so) left. Go ahead and give them some extra time and then start the discussion when everyone seems ready to go.

SET UP FOR THE DISCUSSION

Make sure the seating arrangement is inclusive and encourages a comfortable, safe atmosphere for discussion. Theater-style seating (in rows) isn't discussion-friendly. Instead, arrange the chairs in a circle or semicircle (or sit on the floor with pillows!).

SET BOUNDARIES

It'll be helpful to set a few ground rules before the discussion. Keep the rules to a minimum, of course, but let the kids know what's expected of them. Here are suggestions for some basic ground rules—

- **What's said in this room stays in this room.** Emphasize the importance of confidentiality. Confidentiality is vital for a good discussion. If your kids can't keep the discussion in the room, then they won't open up.
- **No put-downs.** Mutual respect is important. If your kids disagree with some opinions, ask them to comment on the subject (but not on the other person). It's okay to have healthy debate about different ideas, but personal attacks aren't kosher—and they detract from discussion. Communicate that your students can share their thoughts and ideas—even if they may be different or unpopular.
- **There's no such thing as a dumb question.** Your group members must feel free to ask questions at any time. In fact, since MORE HIGH SCHOOL TALKSHEETS digs into a lot of Scripture, you may get hard questions from students that you cannot immediately answer. DON'T PANIC! Affirm that it's a great question, and you aren't sure of the answer—but you'll do some study over the

next week and unpack it next time (and be sure to do this).

- **No one is forced to talk.** Some kids will open up, some won't. Let everyone know they each have the right to pass or not answer any question.
- **Only one person speaks at a time.** This is a mutual respect issue. Everyone's opinion is worthwhile and deserves to be heard.

Communicate with your group that everyone needs to respect these boundaries. If you sense your group members are attacking each other or adopting a negative attitude during the discussion, stop and deal with the problem before going on. Every youth ministry needs to be a safe place where students can freely be who God created them to be without fear.

SET THE STAGE

Always phrase your questions so that you're asking for an opinion, not a be-all, end-all answer. The simple addition of the less-threatening "What do you think…" at the beginning of a question makes it a request for an opinion rather than a demand for the right answer. Your kids will relax when they feel more comfortable and confident. Plus, they'll know you actually care about their opinions, and they'll feel appreciated.

LEAD THE DISCUSSION

Discuss the TalkSheet with the group and encourage all your kids to participate. The more they contribute, the better the discussion will be.

If your youth group is big, you may divide it into smaller groups. Some of the Talksheets request that your students work in smaller groups. Once the smaller groups have completed their discussions, combine them into one large group and ask the different groups to share their ideas.

You don't have to divide the group with every TalkSheet. For some discussions you may want to vary the group size or divide the meeting into groups of the same sex. The discussion should target the questions and answers on the TalkSheet. Go through them and ask the students to share their responses. Have them compare their answers and brainstorm new ones in addition to the ones they've written down.

AFFIRM ALL RESPONSES—RIGHT OR WRONG

Let your kids know that their comments and contributions are appreciated and important. This is especially true for those who rarely speak during group activities. Make a point of thanking them for joining in. This will be an incentive for them to participate further.

Remember that affirmation doesn't mean approval. Affirm even those comments that seem wrong to you. You'll show that everyone has a right to express ideas—no matter how controversial those ideas may be. If someone states an off-base opinion, make a mental note of the comment. Then in your wrap-up, come back to the comment or present a different point of view in a positive way. But don't reprimand the student who voiced the comment.

AVOID GIVING THE AUTHORITATIVE ANSWER

Some kids believe you have the correct answer to every question. They'll look to you for approval, even when they're answering another group member's question. If they start to focus on you for answers, redirect them toward the group by making a comment like, "Remember that you're talking to everyone, not just me."

LISTEN TO EACH PERSON

Good discussion leaders know how to listen. Although it's tempting at times, don't monopolize the discussion. Encourage others to talk first—then express your opinions during your wrap-up.

DON'T FORCE IT

Encourage all your kids to talk, but don't make them comment. Each member has the right to pass. If you feel that the discussion isn't going well, go to the next question or restate the present question to keep things moving.

DON'T TAKE SIDES

Encourage everybody to think through their positions and opinions—ask questions to get them going deeper. If everyone agrees on an issue, you can play devil's advocate with tough questions and stretch their thinking. Remain neutral—your point of view is your own, not that of the group.

DON'T LET ANYONE (INCLUDING YOU) TAKE OVER

Nearly every youth group has one person who likes to talk and is perfectly willing to express an opinion on any subject—*all the time*. Encourage equal participation from all members.

LET THEM LAUGH!

Discussions can be fun! Most of the TalkSheets include questions that'll make students laugh and get them thinking, too. Some of your students' answers will be hilarious—feel free to stop and laugh as a group.

LET THEM BE SILENT

Silence can be scary for discussion leaders! Some react by trying to fill the silence with a question or a comment. The following suggestions may help you to handle silence more effectively—

- **Be comfortable with silence.** Wait it out for 30 seconds or so to respond, which can feel like forever in a group. You may want to restate the question to give your kids a gentle nudge.
- **Talk about the silence with the group.** What does the silence mean? Do they really not have any comments? Maybe they're confused, embarrassed, or don't want to share.
- **Answer the silence with questions or comments like, "I know this is challenging to think about..." or "It's scary to be the first to talk."** If you acknowledge the silence, it may break the ice.
- **Ask a different question that may be easier to handle or that'll clarify the one already posed.** But don't do this too quickly without giving them time to think the first one through.
- **The "two more answers" key.** When you feel like moving on from a question, you may want to ask for two more answers to make sure you've heard all of the great ideas. Many students have good stuff to say, but for one reason or another choose not to share. This key skill may help you draw out some of the best answers before moving on.

KEEP IT UNDER CONTROL

Monitor the discussion. Be aware if the discussion is going in a certain direction or off track. This can happen fast, especially if your students disagree or things get heated. Mediate wisely and set the tone that you want. If your group gets bored with an issue, get them back on track. Let the discussion unfold but be sensitive to your group and who is or isn't getting involved.

If a student brings up a side issue that's interesting, decide whether or not to pursue it. If the discussion is going well and the issue is worth discussing, let them talk it through it. But if things get off track, say something like, "Let's come back to that subject later if we have time. Right now, let's finish our discussion on..."

BE CREATIVE AND FLEXIBLE

If you find other ways to use the TalkSheets, use them! Go ahead and add other questions or Bible references. Don't feel pressured to spend time on every single activity. If you're short on time, you can skip some items. Stick with the questions that are the most interesting to the group.

SET YOUR GOALS

TalkSheets are designed to move along toward a goal, but you need to identify *your* goal in advance. What would you like your youth to learn? What truth should they discover? What's the goal of the session? If you don't know where you're going, it's doubtful you'll get there.

BE THERE FOR YOUR KIDS

Some kids may actually want to talk more with you about a certain topic. (Hey! You got 'em thinking!) Let them know you can talk one-on-one with them afterward.

CLOSE THE DISCUSSION

Present a challenge to the group by asking yourself, "What do I want my students to remember most from this discussion?" There's your wrap-up! It's important to conclude by affirming the group and offering a summary that ties the discussion together.

Sometimes you won't need a wrap-up. You may want to leave the issue hanging and discuss it in another meeting. That way, your group can think about it more and you can nail down the final ideas later.

TAKE IT FURTHER

On the leader's guide page, you'll find additional materials—labeled MORE—that provide extra assistance to you. Some sessions contain an additional activity—e.g., an opener, expanded discussion, or fun idea. Some have support material that can help you handle some potential confusion related to the topic. These aren't a must, but highly recommended. They let the kids reflect upon, evaluate, dig in a bit more, review, and assimilate what they've learned. These activities may lead to even more discussion and better learning.

1. If someone were to videotape a few weeks of your life, what routines or patterns would that person begin to see day after day? In the space provided, list your routines from the time you get up until you go to sleep at night.

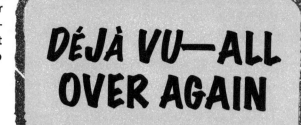

DÉJÀ VU—ALL OVER AGAIN

2. Would you describe your life as quiet or noisy? Why?

3. If you had to use quiet or noisy to describe Jesus' life, which one would you choose? Why?

4. Check out these pairs of verses. What patterns do you see in Jesus' life? Write quiet or noisy next to each reference, depending on which word best describes the situation.

   a. Mark 1:16-34 _____   Mark 1:35-38 _____

   b. Mark 1:40-44 _____   Mark 1:45 _____

   c. Mark 2:1-12 _____   Mark 2:13 _____

   d. Mark 2:13 _____   Mark 2:23 _____

   e. Mark 3:1-6 _____   Mark 3:7 _____

   f. Mark 3:7-12_____   Mark 3:13 _____

   g. Mark 3:20 (first half) _____   Mark 3:20 (second half) _____

   h. Mark 4:10 _____   Mark 4:34 _____

   i. Mark 4:35-36_____   Mark 4:37-41 _____

   j. Mark 5:1 _____   Mark 5:2-20_____

   k. Mark 5:21 (first half) _____   Mark 5:21 (second half) _____

   l. Mark 6:30-32 _____   Mark 6:33-34 _____

5. Describe the routines or patterns being lived out in Jesus' life and the lives of his disciples.

6. List the times and places where you might have some routine patterns of quiet in which to connect with God on a daily basis.

From *Still More High School TalkSheets: 50 Creative Discussions for Your Youth Group* by Dr. David W. Rogers. Permission to reproduce this page granted only for use in buyer's youth group. Copyright © 2009 by Youth Specialties. www.youthspecialties.com

1. *DÉJÀ VU*—ALL OVER AGAIN—Finding quiet moments with God in the routine of noisy lives *(Mark 1–6)*

THIS WEEK

This TalkSheet offers the opportunity to think about the routines of our busy lives while intentionally looking for times when we might grab some quiet moments with God. In the midst of his noisy life, Jesus intentionally sought out time with God but always returned to his responsibilities.

OPENER

Start by talking about the explosion of reality television. Instead of the music videos that launched MTV onto the airwaves, in recent years this channel has done very well by coming up with new reality TV shows that grab our attention. You might want to mention a few shows such as *The Real World*, *Road Rules*, and *Survivor*, as well as home-improvement reality shows such as *Extreme Makeover: Home Edition* or *Flip This House*. Now ask your group members to name as many reality TV shows as they can think of while you write their responses on a whiteboard or large sheet of paper. When they've exhausted their ideas, turn their attention to the TalkSheet.

THE DISCUSSION, BY NUMBERS

1. Ask your group to think about what people would see if someone were to record their lives 24/7 like in a reality TV show. As they think about this question, ask them to jot down the routines that people would see if their "reality show" aired.

2. Your students' lives are no doubt busy, yet full of routines. Mention some of the routines that are present in most people's lives, regardless of their season of life (eating breakfast, going to school or work, and so on). Now ask them to describe their lives as *quiet* or *noisy* and explain their choices. Ask for volunteers to share their responses.

3. Now shift the discussion to how they'd describe Jesus' life—*quiet* or *noisy*—and why. Allow a few students to share their thoughts. Some may say "both," which isn't a bad thing.

4. Divide up the 12 pairs of Scripture passages among your students. After they look up their two passages, they should indicate whether they could be described as noisy or quiet. Go around and have them share their answers and why they chose them. The students who aren't sharing should write the answers in the blanks on their own TalkSheets.

5. There's a pattern of all kinds of noisy responsibilities followed by intentional times of quiet (even brief moments of quiet). The quiet moments include getting up early and heading to a mountain, taking a boat ride, walking through a grain field, or taking a stroll by the water. Jesus' routine of intentionally seeking a few moments away from the crowds in order to catch his breath with God is a great example for us. Mention how the Hebrew word *Sabbath* can be translated "catching one's breath." Then ask them to think about the following question as they prepare to finish the TalkSheet: "What would it look like for you to remember the Sabbath by *catching your breath* with God every day?"

6. Take a few minutes to wrap up your time by going over some of their answers. Help them to think creatively about quiet moments in their day when they could routinely "catch their breath" with God, such as riding in the car, taking a walk before doing their homework, stretching before they work out, or taking a shower.

THE CLOSE

Reiterate the importance of reading the Bible, praying, and investing in some quiet moments alone with God each day. Then read Hebrews 11:6, which promises that God "rewards those who earnestly seek him." For the week ahead, ask the students to read (from their TalkSheets) two passages from Mark in the mornings and again in the evenings to remind them of the patterns of Jesus' life. Challenge them to seek out a few moments of *quiet* with God every day.

MORE

• Watch *Groundhog Day* as a group and discuss the patterns of Phil Connors' (played by Bill Murray) life and how his routine might relate to their own lives. Screen the movie ahead of time for anything that might be offensive to your group or their parents.

• Create a montage of clips from reality TV shows to play for your group at the beginning of your time together.

• Discuss what your students do when they have quiet moments alone with God. What works for them? What doesn't?

1. If you could have five things that would set you apart as "rich," what would they be?

GIMME FIVE

2. What things make someone a good friend?

3. The thing I value most in a friendship is...

4. The thing that turns me off more than anything in a friendship is...

5. Describe a time when being with your friends made a difficult or sad situation easier.

6. What's the most memorable thing a friend ever did for you?

7. What's the most memorable thing you ever did for a friend?

8. According to John 15:12-15, what value does Jesus place on his friends?

9. If the goal of our lives is to become more like Jesus, how do the following verses challenge you to be the kind of friend God desires?

   • Proverbs 17:17

   • Proverbs 18:24

   • Proverbs 27:6

From *Still More High School TalkSheets: 50 Creative Discussions for Your Youth Group* by Dr. David W. Rogers. Permission to reproduce this page granted only for use in buyer's youth group. Copyright © 2009 by Youth Specialties. www.youthspecialties.com

THIS WEEK
In this TalkSheet your students will discuss the value and characteristics of a good friend. They'll also learn that God created us to live in relationships with one another. In order to have good friends, one must choose to be a good friend.

OPENER
Start by asking your group to name some of the richest people in the world. If they need help, suggest professional athletes, business people, royalty, movie stars, and so on. After they give you a few answers, tell your group that surveys suggest that the number one goal of many people is to be rich and famous.

THE DISCUSSION, BY NUMBERS
1. Ask them to write down five things that would set them apart as a rich person. Then take a few minutes and have them share what they wrote. After everyone has had a turn, say, **It's been said that a rich person is one who can count five people as good friends.** Based on this statement, ask them to think to themselves (not out loud) whether they can consider themselves rich.
2. Have your group answer questions two, three, and four. Then call on a few students and ask them to share all three of their answers.
3. See question two.
4. See question two.
5. Be sensitive to what's shared, as some stories may be painful. Also keep in mind that some students may not feel like they have any friends and might find this discussion difficult. Don't assume that all of your students have great friendships. If necessary, share one of your own experiences to get the discussion going.
6. If you're running low on time, ask your students to text or email their answers to you later in the week. Otherwise, have them answer questions six and seven together and ask a few volunteers to share.
7. See question six.

8. Have your group turn to John 15:12-15 and ask a student to read it out loud. Encourage them to think deeper than they have before. Take your time in moderating this part of the discussion and allow them to dig around in their thoughts about the passage and what they know about Jesus and his disciples, whom he's now calling his "friends."
9. Now ask three volunteers to read Proverbs 17:17, 18:24, and 27:6. Pause after each verse is read and ask the group to consider what the verse means to them. Encourage your students to move beyond reciting the "right" answer and respond to the question in a more personal way. Give everyone a chance to share before you move on to The Close.

THE CLOSE
Ask them to write down the statement from earlier in the discussion: "It's been said that a rich person is one who can count five people as good friends." Challenge them to take another look at their TalkSheet answers and reevaluate if they're "rich." Then encourage them to be the type of friend God desires them to be and to commit to pray for their friends. Close by praying over your group. Ask God to give each of them at least one really good friend and help them to be a good friend to someone.

MORE
• **Discuss with your group what it means to be a friend—**
    a. **By what you say (James 3:5-11, Matthew 12:36-37)**
    b. **By what you do (Mark 10:45, John 13:1-17)**
    c. **By what you carry (Galatians 6:2, Psalm 55:22)**
• **Watch an episode of *Friends* together. Be careful to screen the episode for anything that might be offensive to your group or their parents.**

1. **Create a Top-10 list of things you'd never do in public.**

   10.

   9.

   8.

   7.

   6.

   5.

   4.

   3.

   2.

   1.

SHOCK VALUE!

2. **Jesus told a jaw-dropping story found in Luke 15:1, 11-32. His parable described some things that people in his day would never do in public. Why would his audience shake their heads at these things?**

   • v. 12: A younger son asks his father for his inheritance.

   • v. 12: A father divides his property between his sons.

   • vv. 13, 30: The younger son squanders all he had.

   • v. 15: The younger son feeds pigs.

   • v. 18: The younger son decides to go back home to his father.

   • v. 20: The father ran to meet his son.

   • v. 29: The older son confronts his father.

3. **Why do you think Jesus told a story that had so many elements that would never have been done in public back in the first century?**

4. **What do you think Jesus wants you to take away from this story and apply to your life?**

5. **In what ways have you been insensitive or demanding of your parents and need to confess, repent, and ask for forgiveness?**

6. **Because of this discussion, I'm going to _____.**

From *Still More High School TalkSheets: 50 Creative Discussions for Your Youth Group* by Dr. David W. Rogers. Permission to reproduce this page granted only for use in buyer's youth group. Copyright © 2009 by Youth Specialties. www.youthspecialties.com

THIS WEEK

This TalkSheet centers on the parable of the lost son. Your students will consider the elements of Jesus' story from the cultural vantage point of his first-century audience. Jesus was a master storyteller, and this parable certainly would have created a buzz.

OPENER

Start by sharing a few examples of things you'd never do in public, such as pick your nose or tell a joke in the middle of a funeral. After you have them thinking about such things, ask your group to consider a top 10 list of things they'd never do in public.

THE DISCUSSION, BY NUMBERS

1. Divide your students into teams of two or three to foster more creativity, but tell them to keep it clean. After they've shared their lists, consider asking the group to vote on the absolute number-one thing they'd never do in public.

2. Point out that "public no-no's" in one culture may be totally innocent in another. Then ask your group to turn to Luke 15:1, 11-32. Read the story out loud and have the students fill in their answers.

   - (v. 12: A younger son asks his father for his inheritance.) First, such a request would be viewed as the younger son putting a curse on his father: "I wish you were dead so I could have my part of your money." Second, there was huge cultural significance on the *oldest* male heir receiving the birthrights and blessings. (Genesis 25:31, Genesis 27:1-45, Genesis 29:32, Genesis 49:3, Exodus 12:29, Deuteronomy 21:17)
   - (v. 12: A father divides his property between his sons.) A first-century Jewish father would view this request as a public insult and never agree to it. It would result in immense shame on both the eldest son and the father.
   - (vv. 13, 30: The younger son squanders all he had.) The younger son hocked his inheritance for cash and went on a sinful spending spree in a foreign country, which further insulted his father. (Proverbs 5:8-10, Proverbs 29:3)
   - (v. 15: The younger son feeds pigs.) Pigs were considered unclean by Jewish religious standards. Most Jews would rather die than take such a job. (Leviticus 11:7, Isaiah 65:1-4, Isaiah 66:3, 17)

   - (v. 18: The younger son decides to go back home to his father.) Although the thought may have entered the son's mind, he never would have followed through. The younger son would be considered dead to his family and community. (Leviticus 26:40-45, Jeremiah 3:12-15, 1 John 1:9)
   - (v. 20: The father ran to meet his son.) Elders were respected and acted with much dignity—elders didn't run. So when Jesus described the father racing to his son with a loving embrace, the crowd saw the father as acting undignified. (Genesis 45:14-15, Genesis 46:29)
   - (v. 29: The older son confronts his father.) The older son shames his father by reprimanding him for his gracious actions toward his little brother.

3. Jesus knew his audience would be astute enough to filter this story through the lens of the Old Testament teaching. It would impact his audience's view of God—sinful and shameful people *could* have a relationship with a God of love and forgiveness.

4. There are no wrong answers. However, one main conclusion should be drawn: Nothing we do is so shocking that God wouldn't run toward us with open arms of love and forgiveness.

5. Perhaps this would be a good time to move the discussion toward how your students treat their parents.

6. Ask your group to complete the sentence as an action step they'll take in response to the discussion.

THE CLOSE

Remind the group of how powerful stories can be. Jesus always has a purpose in the stories, words, and actions of his life. If we put ourselves in the sandals of his first-century audience, we may view things in a whole new way.

MORE

- **Have some of your students look up the additional Scripture references in question two on your sheet to get a better picture of the story Jesus was alluding to.**
- **Talk about how Jesus' audience would have viewed this parable as a parallel to the story of Israel going into exile and coming home again by the mercy of God. Those who longed to experience the liberation of Israel would love to hear such a story.**
- **A second Top-10 list could focus on things you'd never do in front of your parents. You could even talk about embarrassing moments that have occurred.**

1. Write down as many people as you can think of who have the name "John." These are just "Johns" you know of or know something about but don't necessarily know well.

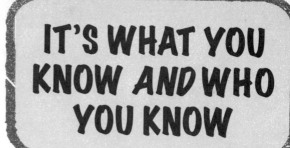

2. Now write down all the people with the name "John" that you do know well.

3. List what caused you to place some "Johns" on the first list (you don't know them well) and other "Johns" on the second list (you do know them well).

4. If you had to put Jesus on list one or list two, which list would you put him on and why?

5. What would it take for you to place Jesus' name on the other list?

6. Check out John 14:7. Which list do you think Jesus was referring to as he talked with his disciples about "knowing him" and "knowing my Father"?

7. If you had to come up with an approach to develop *oida* (intimate knowledge) of Jesus, what would be involved? What would it look like lived out over a week, a month, a year?

8. What's one aspect of the approach to knowing—to developing an *oida* of—Jesus that you'd be willing to live out this week?

From *Still More High School TalkSheets: 50 Creative Discussions for Your Youth Group* by Dr. David W. Rogers. Permission to reproduce this page granted only for use in buyer's youth group. Copyright © 2009 by Youth Specialties. www.youthspecialties.com

4. IT'S WHAT YOU KNOW *AND* WHO YOU KNOW—Allowing basic Bible knowledge
to move us toward intimacy with God *(John 14:7)*

THIS WEEK
Your group will look at the "It's not what you know, it's who you know" philosophy from Jesus' point of view. They'll eavesdrop on part of a conversation Jesus had with his closest friends and find out that life is both what you know as well as who you know.

OPENER
Help your group define the difference between *knowing about* someone and *knowing* someone. Give examples of famous people you know about, such as athletes or movie stars. (The more details you can give, the better.) Then make the point that although you may know *about* a person, you may not know them at all. Now give an example of someone you know intimately, such as your spouse, a family member, or a close friend before turning your students' attention to the TalkSheet.

THE DISCUSSION, BY NUMBERS
1. This first list can be "Johns" they've never met, have only heard about, or seen on TV. After you've given them a few minutes, ask them to share with the group. Write all the names on a whiteboard to create a little energy and give it a feeling of competition.
2. Now shift the focus to the "Johns" they know well. Have them share these names with the group.
3. Ask your group to jot down the factors that determined which list their "Johns" went on. Some answers may be similar to what you've already mentioned. That's fine. The object is to get them thinking about the differences in the two kinds of knowing.
4. Now ask which list Jesus belongs on, based on the criteria they just described. By a show of hands, see who put Jesus on list one and who put Jesus on list two. Remind them that it's better to be real than to tell the group what they think it wants to hear.
5. Rather than talk about why they put Jesus' name on a specific list, ask them what it would take for them to put Jesus' name on list two.
6. Have your group turn to John 14:7. It's part of a conversation Jesus had with his disciples. Have your group fill out question six and then ask them to share their answers. Explain how Jesus uses two words that are translated as "know" in English, but have different definitions in Greek. "If you really knew (*ginosko*) me, you would have known (*oida*) my Father as well." *Ginosko* simply means "basic knowledge" (or "basic Bible knowledge" for our purposes). *Oida* means "a relational knowledge" or "an intimate knowledge." It's like Jesus is saying, "If you'd grasped the basic Bible knowledge about me, then you'd have a relational intimacy in knowing God the Father." Thus, "It's what you know, *and* it's who you know."

7. Ask them to come up with an approach for developing that same type of *oida* knowledge of Jesus. According to Jesus, one of the ways to get to "it's who you know (*oida*)" is based on "it's what you know (*ginosko*)." Ask the group to share their plans and then formulate an overall approach using everyone's input. Ask what a person's relationship with God might look like next week, next month, and next year if they were to implement this approach to knowing God.

8. Finish the discussion by asking the group to consider the elements that were just discussed. Ask each person to commit to implementing one of those elements this week as they pursue an *oida* knowing of God. Ask for volunteers to share what they wrote and how they'll do their best to implement it.

THE CLOSE
As you close remind your group that relationships require consistent care and constant maintenance. They don't happen overnight. They must be pursued and cultivated. Challenge them to read John 14 each day and memorize verse 7.

MORE
• **Divide the group into teams and have a Bible trivia competition. The first team to get 10 questions right is the winner. Focus on basic Bible knowledge, such as naming the Ten Commandments, Jesus' disciples, and what Adam and Eve ate in the garden.**
• **Challenge your group to commit to trying an agreed-upon approach to knowing God better by engaging in spiritual disciplines, such as Bible reading, daily prayer, serving others, sharing their faith, fasting, and silence.**
• **Ask your group to set goals for basic Bible knowledge they'd like to acquire by next week, next month, and next year. How do they see these goals changing their relationship with God?**

1. List as many pairs of incompatible (don't go together) things as you can think of.

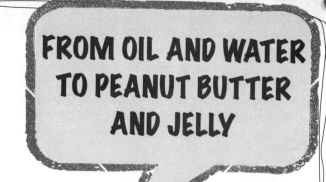

FROM OIL AND WATER TO PEANUT BUTTER AND JELLY

2. Now list as many pairs of compatible (do go together) things as you can think of.

3. What makes something compatible or incompatible with something else?

4. Check out Isaiah 11:6-9 and list the various pairings of traditionally incompatible subjects. Beside your list of groupings, jot down why you think they're normally seen as being incompatible with one another.

5. Why is it important for God to reconcile and restore subjects that have traditionally been incompatible with each other?

6. What are some examples of places where there's incompatibility between people or between issues in your life and the lives of your friends?

    a. Your family

    b. Your community or school

    c. Your world

7. What does God want you to do as a part of the solution for the reconciliation and restoration of incompatibility among the examples you listed in question six?

From *Still More High School TalkSheets: 50 Creative Discussions for Your Youth Group* by Dr. David W. Rogers. Permission to reproduce this page granted only for use in buyer's youth group. Copyright © 2009 by Youth Specialties. *www.youthspecialties.com*

THIS WEEK
This week your group will look at a Messianic passage found in Isaiah 11:6-9. The discussion will help your students identify incompatible relationships in their lives and the world. It will also challenge them to think about how God might want them to be a part of the reconciliation process.

OPENER
After your group gathers, add a little bit of light oil to a clear container filled with water. The oil should settle on the surface. (Be sure to test it beforehand.) Then take a couple pieces of bread—one with peanut butter, and one with jelly—and make a PB&J sandwich. As you carry out these object lessons, talk about how some things in life are incompatible (don't go together) like oil and water, and some things are compatible (go together) like PB&J.

THE DISCUSSION, BY NUMBERS
1. Now that your group is thinking about compatibility, challenge them to see how many groupings they can come up with that are *not* compatible with one another on question one and then go right into making their list of compatible groupings for question two. Feel free to tweak this however you want to suit your group. You can let them make up things or focus them toward more traditional incompatible pairings such as oil and water or cats and dogs, and PB&J or peas and carrots for compatible examples. Feel free to create teams and make it a contest. After they have their answers written down for questions one and two, let them share what they came up with.
2. See question one.
3. Challenge your group to think through the "why" part of their lists on the first two questions. What made those two things appear together? Answers might include preference, chemical makeup, worldview, political alignment, economics, cultural tradition, racial stereotypes, learned behaviors, or religious conviction, just to name a few. This question requires your students to think. If you can get them engaged and thinking a bit deeper, it will make the rest of the discussion more fruitful.
4. Now move your group's attention to a listing of traditionally incompatible subjects found in Isaiah

11:6-9. Have your group read this passage of Scripture and make a list of the incompatible subjects listed. Then have your group discuss what makes those relationships incompatible.
5. It shouldn't take long for your group to talk about why the subjects listed in the previous question are traditionally incompatible. Be ready to nudge them to talk a bit more about why they believe it's important to God that restoration and reconciliation take place in relationships. If it's something on God's heart, how should that inform the way we seek relational restoration and reconciliation?
6. Have your group continue talking through these issues of reconciling and restoring relationships to compatibility with your group. Have them consider their own lives and places where there may be existing incompatibility in the following areas: (a) family, (b) community or school, and (c) the world. Have them write down their insights before talking through each section.
7. Encourage your group to consider some of the steps they can take to be a part of the compatibility solution, rather than experiencing only the problem of incompatibility. Challenge your group to not only get creative in their possible solutions, but also to follow through with some of their ideas.

THE CLOSE
Break out a loaf of bread, a jar of peanut butter, a jar of jelly, and enjoy making and eating some peanut butter and jelly sandwiches to wrap up your time together.

MORE
- Have a compatible-incompatible scavenger hunt. Take your group to a local mall, large discount store (like Wal-Mart), or grocery store. Divide them into teams and give each team a $10 limit to buy as many compatible or incompatible objects as they can find (and afford) in 30 minutes. Designate a rendezvous point and see who came up with the most items for their $10 limit.
- Host a compatibility feast for your group. Provide a mixture of items that "go together," such as milk and cookies, and enjoy eating and fellowshipping with your group.
- Have a panel discussion with community leaders who can speak to issues where local, national, and global reconciliation or restoration need to take place and how high school students can be a part of the process.

1. What are the biggest secrets that have been made public?

SECRETS

2. What motivates a person to keep something a secret?

3. How might people react when their secret is exposed?

4. Check out Exodus 2:11-15. What was Moses' secret?

5. How did he try to keep his secret hidden?

6. How did he respond when his secret was exposed? Why?

7. Would you expose your secret if you knew no one would find out it was your secret?

8. What do you think God wants you do with your secret? Why?

From *Still More High School TalkSheets: 50 Creative Discussions for Your Youth Group* by Dr. David W. Rogers. Permission to reproduce this page granted only for use in buyer's youth group. Copyright © 2009 by Youth Specialties. *www.youthspecialties.com*

6. SECRETS—Dealing with the hidden things in our lives *(Exodus 2:11-15)*

THIS WEEK
Humans have tried to keep certain things in their lives hidden ever since Adam and Eve hid from God. Today, your group will look at the subject of secrets and see that even a great hero of the Old Testament tried to keep a secret "hidden in the sand."

OPENER
Tell the story of Frank Warren, founder of PostSecret. In 2004, he gave blank postcards (addressed to his home) to strangers and left them in public places with instructions to decorate one side of the postcard, write down a secret they've never told anyone, and mail it. Literally thousands of decorated postcards arrived in the mail, and secrets continue to arrive today. Some of the postcards can be seen in Frank's books, and the most recent ones are posted at *www.post-secret.com*. Share a few with your students and then move on to the TalkSheet. (Some of the images may not be appropriate for your group.)

THE DISCUSSION, BY NUMBERS
1. Help them think outside the box. One big "secret" might be how the world was thought to be flat. Others might involve discoveries in science, new inventions, or medical breakthroughs. Don't invest too much time on this one. It's just to get them thinking about the subject.
2. Generate some deeper discussion and get them thinking about *why* people desire to cloak things in secrecy—fear, embarrassment, pain, sin, or anonymity.
3. Possible reactions to the exposure of secrets might be crying, lying, running away, violence, laughing, embarrassment, or even revenge. Set up question four by saying something like, **Did you know that even Bible heroes had secrets? When you think of Moses, probably the last thing that comes to mind is, "Here's a guy with a secret." Let's check it out.**
4. Have someone read Exodus 2:11-15 out loud. Then ask your group to jot down Moses' secret. (He killed an Egyptian and buried him in the sand.)
5. Verse 12 shows that Moses was "glancing this way and that" before he struck the Egyptian, and then he tried to hide the body in the sand. Ask the students what they would've done if they'd been in Moses' sandals.
6. Verse 14 tells us Moses panicked and fled to another country in verse 15. Challenge them to think about why. Point out how Exodus 2:2 says that when Moses was just a baby, his mother "hid him for three months." Some traits may be passed down from generation to generation, but God expects people to be accountable for their own actions. Subtly shift the focus from Moses' reaction to how your students react when a secret is exposed. Challenge them to be vulnerable.
7. Say, **We all have secrets we'd like to keep hidden. One reason PostSecret is so successful is because people can expose a secret without being found out. There's a great sense of relief when you can share a secret anonymously.** Ask if your students would share their secrets if they knew they wouldn't be found out. After each person has responded, ask if anybody has a secret they'd like to uncover before the group today.
8. Your students need to answer the last question for themselves: What does God want them do with their secrets? Should they hold on to them or share them with someone? Point out that some secrets need to be shared with a safe adult, such as a pastor, parent, or counselor. If someone has abused them, it's vital that they tell someone so healing can occur.

THE CLOSE
Pass out blank postcards (addressed to you) and encourage your group to take them home, write a secret, and mail them to you anonymously. Tell them you'll pray for the sender of each postcard you receive. Then remind your students that you're always available if they ever need a safe person to confide in. Close by praying that your students will deal with their secrets in a godly way.

MORE
• Take it a step further and begin your own PostSecret art project with your group. Dedicate a space in your meeting area to display some of the secrets.
• Have students write their secrets on postcards before doing something symbolic with them, such as placing them at the foot of a cross or burning them in a fireplace, to demonstrate that they've dealt with the secret.
• Have a professional youth counselor on hand for students who want or need professional help in dealing with their secrets.

1. The most extreme person I know is
   _____ because…

2. The most extreme thing I've ever done is…

3. The most extreme thing I'd like to do in my lifetime is…

EXTREME BALANCE

4. How would you describe someone who lives a life of balance?

5. List some examples of people who take a balanced approach to life.

6. Which approach (extreme or balanced) does God want you to take in life and why?

7. If you had to describe Jesus as being either extreme or balanced, which word would you choose and why?

8. Check out Revelation 3:15-16 and Ecclesiastes 7:15-18. Based on these two passages, which approach to life does God desire from you: Extreme or balanced? Why?

9. What's one area of your life in which you need to become more extreme and one area in which you need to have more balance?

   Extreme:

   Balance:

From *Still More High School TalkSheets: 50 Creative Discussions for Your Youth Group* by Dr. David W. Rogers. Permission to reproduce this page granted only for use in buyer's youth group. Copyright © 2009 by Youth Specialties. www.youthspecialties.com

7. EXTREME BALANCE—Exploring God's desired approach to life
(Ecclesiastes 7:15-18, Revelation 3:15-16)

THIS WEEK
With the advent of the X Games, it seems anything can be taken to extreme levels. Yet living with balance is also valued in our culture. This discussion will look at how God wants his followers to approach life. Are we to be extreme, balanced, or both?

OPENER
This opener requires a bit of preparation. Feel free to adapt the concept to fit your own circumstances. You'll need at least two large frozen drinks for contestants to drink quickly. You'll also need two Atomic Fireball candies for contestants to hold in their mouths. The gist of this competition is to see who can endure the extreme conditions the longest. Choose guys versus girls or one grade versus another and let the extreme hot-cold competition begin.

THE DISCUSSION, BY NUMBERS
1. Have your students complete questions one through three before asking each person to share all three responses with the group.
2. See question one.
3. See question one.
4. Let the group know you're going to go to the opposite end of the spectrum for a few minutes and talk about what it means to be balanced. Give them a few minutes to think and share their answers with the group.
5. Ask them to list people (occupations) with a balanced approach to life, such as surgeons, government officials, and judges. Let them share their ideas with the group.
6. In a way questions six and seven are trick questions, since a case can be made for both. However, let your students make a decision before giving their explanation as to why they chose extreme or balanced.
7. Encourage them to think about some of Jesus' teachings and how he lived his life. He had some pretty radical teachings (extreme). But he was gentle with children one minute and confronting religious officials the next (balanced).
8. The Revelation 3:14-15 passage is meant to be an example of extremes. (It should also allow you to refer back to the hot-and-cold competition.) In this passage Jesus is admonishing the church in Laodicea for becoming lukewarm in their devotion to God. Ecclesiastes 7:15-18 references two extreme approaches to life: Being overly righteous and being wicked. Solomon ends the passage by advising: "Whoever fears God will avoid all [extremes]." This Hebrew phrase can also be translated: "Whoever fears God will follow them both." In other words, Solomon is calling for balance. Be cautious of becoming "so heavenly minded that you're no earthly good." At the same time, beware of letting the world overtake your life so people have no idea you're a follower of Jesus. The key to becoming a mature Christ-follower is to live passionately while not becoming a religious extremist who repels people. Jesus was extreme in his mission, yet gentle, kind, loving, gracious, wise, and generous to all he came in contact with. Jesus' approach to life was one of extreme balance.
9. The final question will help them zero in on their own lives. Give them a few minutes to think about what God desires and share with the group.

THE CLOSE
Ask your students to split off into groups of two or three and conclude the time by having them pray for one another in the areas they just shared with the group. Encourage them to exchange contact information so they can check in with each other to see how things are going when it comes to extremes and balance in their lives.

MORE
• Gather the group for an X Games watching party. Many video stores carry extreme sports videos you can rent.
• Create your own Extreme Games and have your students participate for prizes. Events might include extreme jump rope, extreme relay races, and extreme egg toss or water balloon toss. Get creative and let your kids make up the events and the rules.
• Have the group play games that require good balance, such as balancing items on your head or on a spoon during a relay race. You could even rent inflatable sumo wrestler suits and let the students test their balance in the sumo ring. Let the students come up with the balance events.

1. Besides the "Hokey Pokey," list as many dances as you can think of.

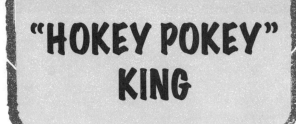

2. What makes the "Hokey Pokey" so hokey?

3. Check out 2 Samuel 6:14-22. What was taking place and how did David respond to the situation?

4. Now read 2 Samuel 11:1-26. Why might the "Hokey Pokey" be David's dance of choice for this chapter?

5. What was the progression of "David's sin dance"?

  • v. 1

  • v. 2

  • v. 3

  • v. 4

  • v. 5

  • vv. 6-11

  • vv. 12-13

  • vv. 14-16

  • v. 17

  • v. 25

6. What's one situation in the world today that could be compared to a modern-day "Hokey Pokey" dance (one sin leading to another and another)?

7. What's one area of your life that could potentially become the start to your own "Hokey Pokey" sin dance if you were to "put your right arm in" just to flirt with that sin?

8. What's your strategy for ensuring you won't participate in that "Hokey Pokey" dance?

From *Still More High School TalkSheets: 50 Creative Discussions for Your Youth Group* by Dr. David W. Rogers. Permission to reproduce this page granted only for use in buyer's youth group. Copyright © 2009 by Youth Specialties. www.youthspecialties.com

THIS WEEK

This TalkSheet is about King David and how he moved from dancing before the Ark of the Covenant to committing adultery with Bathsheba. Like with the "Hokey Pokey," David got caught up in the progressive "sin dance." It begins with just an arm or a leg, but it ultimately affects the "whole self."

OPENER

Start by having your group do the "Hokey Pokey." If they're hesitant, ask for volunteers and make it a judged competition, letting their peers vote for the person with the most artistic expression. After the dance is finished and a "Hokey Pokey Artiste" has been crowned, move on to the TalkSheet.

THE DISCUSSION, BY NUMBERS

1. Have the group name some dances. This can be part of the earlier competition. Award extra points to those who demonstrate them.
2. Obviously, there's no right or wrong answer. However, point out that the progression of the song is a bit hokey. (Starting with one body part and adding more until you put your "whole self" in is a great metaphor for the progression of sin. Don't make that connection now. Just know that's where you're headed in the discussion.)
3. David's response to the return of the Ark of the Covenant was to dance.
4. Before you read the story with your group, let them know that if David were to do a dance in accordance with 2 Samuel 11, it would be the "Hokey Pokey." Afterward, explain how the progression of sin in David's life ultimately consumed his "whole self" in the plot to cover up his affair with Bathsheba.
5. Have your group walk through the "dance steps" of David's actions.
   - v. 1: David should have been at war. (Sin often happens when we aren't where we're supposed to be.)
   - v. 2: David's sin wasn't that he saw Bathsheba bathing, but that he looked long enough to know she was "beautiful." (When temptation "appears before our very eyes," our next move—to continue looking or turn away—is critical.)
   - v. 3: David involved someone else in his sin. (Our sin rarely involves just us.) David learned the woman was married.
   - v. 4: David sent messengers to retrieve Bathsheba and had an affair with her.
   - v. 5: Bathsheba is now pregnant and must lie about her pregnancy. However, the Bible makes no indication that Bathsheba put up a fight.
   - vv. 6-11: David brought Uriah home from battle and gave him every opportunity to sleep with his wife. However, Uriah is a man of honor and wouldn't do it.
   - vv. 12-13: David got Uriah drunk so he'd go to bed with Bathsheba. Uriah passed out on his mat.
   - vv. 14-16: David sent Uriah back to war with a death wish, and Joab must carry out the king's orders to sacrifice Uriah's life.
   - v. 17: David's command to Joab ended not only Uriah's life, but also the lives of other soldiers.
   - v. 25: David ended the chapter doing more damage control with both the messenger and Joab.
6. Now help your students apply the progression of the "Hokey Pokey" sin dance to their world today. One example might be the progression of drug use, going from accepting a free sample from a dealer or trying something at a party to an addiction to stealing to support the habit to even jail or death. Let the students share their own scenarios.
7. Ask them to share an area from their own lives that could potentially be a dangerous dance step into their own "Hokey Pokey" sin dance. Ask them to be courageous in sharing their answers. Or have them break off into smaller, same-sex groups to discuss it.
8. Challenge them to come up with a strategy for avoiding the sin dance. Things such as accountability, prayer, memorizing Scripture, church, and hanging out with friends who will influence them toward good dance steps could all be included.

THE CLOSE

Wrap up your time by doing a big group "Hokey Pokey" before closing with prayer.

MORE

- **Have a dance competition with as many dances as your group can think of, such as the twist, the jitterbug, square-dancing, break dancing, line dancing, and so on.**
- **Show clean clips from movies with different dances in them, such as *Saturday Night Fever, Dirty Dancing, Footloose, Fame, Grease,* and *Can't Buy Me Love.***
- **Have a video game competition. Set up some TVs with dance-themed video games, such as Dance Dance Revolution, and see who has the best moves.**

1. How many text messages do you send in a...

    Day:

    Week:

    Month:

RETURN TO SENDER

2. The person I send the most text messages to on a typical day is...

3. The person who sends me the most text messages on a typical day is...

4. What's the most significant thing about being the sender of something?

5. In 2 Samuel 11, describe what's going on with all of the "sending" and "being sent."

    • v. 1

    • v. 3

    • v. 4

    • v. 5

    • v. 6

    • v. 8

    • v. 12

    • v. 14

    • v. 18

    • v. 27

6. From the progression of "sendings" in this chapter, what characteristic do you see emerging in David's life?

7. In what areas of your life are you a "sender"?

8. What's significant about the "send" in 2 Samuel 12:1?

From *Still More High School TalkSheets: 50 Creative Discussions for Your Youth Group* by Dr. David W. Rogers. Permission to reproduce this page granted only for use in buyer's youth group. Copyright © 2009 by Youth Specialties. *www.youthspecialties.com*

THIS WEEK

Whoever "hits the send button" usually believes he's in control of the situation (like David). However, God has a "send button," too. And when we have no accountability in our lives, God will send the right person at the right time to help a "sinning sender" get back on track.

OPENER

Ask your students to see how fast they can text the following message to you and three other people (not in the room): I'M PRAYING FOR YOU TODAY. GOD BLESS! They should begin typing on your count of three. After receiving the first text, have the winner show you their other three "Sent" messages. Ask the students to put their cell phones away and take a look at the TalkSheet.

THE DISCUSSION, BY NUMBERS

1. Have them answer this question honestly. Then identify who has the most and the least in these three time frames: Daily, weekly, and monthly. Remember, the emphasis is on how many texts they *send*.
2. Have them answer questions two and three together and share their answers with the group.
3. See question two.
4. Challenge them to think deeply about this question. The person who sends the message has all kinds of power regarding what's sent, to whom it's sent, the tone of the message, and so on. But with power comes responsibility.
5. Have your group members read 2 Samuel 11 and underline every instance of the words *send* or *sent*. Then have them jot down what's going on each time that word is used. Walk through the story with them and emphasize the sending that takes place.
   - v. 1: David **sent** Joab to fight with the army.
   - v. 3: David **sent** someone to find out who was bathing on the roof.
   - v. 4: David **sent** his servants to get Bathsheba. So far, David feels in control and he's using his power—right or wrong.
   - v. 5: Bathsheba's **sends** word to David: She's pregnant. Perhaps David now felt a bit out of control.
   - v. 6: David tries to cover up his sin. He **sends** a message to Joab, asking him to **send** Bathsheba's husband home. David hopes Uriah will sleep with Bathsheba.
   - v. 8: David **sends** Uriah a welcome-home gift. The manipulation continues.
   - v. 12: David tells Uriah he'll soon be **sent** back to battle. Perhaps Uriah will have a quick rendezvous with his wife? David gets Uriah drunk, just to help things along. The sender continues to work his magic but to no avail.
   - v. 14: David **sends** a letter to Joab, which is basically Uriah's death warrant. Murder is now part of the cover-up plan.
   - v. 18: Joab **sends** word of Uriah's death.
   - v. 27: Bathsheba finishes mourning, and David **sends** for her. She becomes his wife. And it greatly displeases God. (That's never a good description.)
6. Help your students see that when people of power and influence have little or no accountability, they often become manipulative and abusive in their power. David didn't have anyone to hold him accountable. He became a manipulative, power-hungry, control freak who was only interested in his own pleasure. This led him to commit adultery and murder, while still trying to protect his reputation.
7. You want them to talk about points in their lives that could be potential weaknesses if left without any accountability. For David, it was lust and sexual sin that morphed into image management, manipulation, and murder. Encourage honesty and be ready to share one of your own, if necessary.
8. God can be a sender, too. God sent Nathan the prophet to confront David and lead him to repentance. When we become the "sinning sender," God sends people into our lives who will say the hard things when we need to hear them.

CLOSE

Someone needed to confront David about his "sending" problem. Nathan told King David a story that paralleled David's sinful actions. When David angrily pronounced judgment on the sinful man, Nathan basically held up a mirror to David's face. Remind your group that we all need a Nathan in our lives. Challenge them to find someone to hold them accountable.

MORE

- Take a look at Psalm 51—the prayer David prayed after Nathan's visit.
- Compare David's prayer in Psalm 32 with that of Psalm 51 as it relates to 2 Samuel 11–12.
- Have your group come up with a list of questions for accountability partners to use. Then encourage your group to work through the questions with a friend this week.

1. What's the most dangerous situation you and your friends have ever been in together?

2. The time in my life when I felt the closest to God was…

3. The time in my life when I felt the farthest away from God was…

4. Listen to the song "Where You Are" by Rich Mullins. Which Bible story (mentioned in the song) do you relate to the most and why?
   • Daniel in the lions' den (Daniel 6)

   • Jonah in the belly of the fish (Jonah 1–2)

   • Shadrach, Meshach, and Abednego and the blazing furnace (Daniel 3)

5. The song speaks of meeting God "in your time of trial" and in "your hour of prayer." What's the biggest trial you're facing? What time of day are you most likely to pray?

6. Read Romans 8:35-39. What word or phrase in that passage best describes the way you feel about God today? Why?

7. How does knowing that Jesus is with you affect the way you approach difficult situations?

8. Rich Mullins sings about how we can "reach out" to God. How do you do that?

From *Still More High School TalkSheets: 50 Creative Discussions for Your Youth Group* by Dr. David W. Rogers. Permission to reproduce this page granted only for use in buyer's youth group. Copyright © 2009 by Youth Specialties. www.youthspecialties.com

THIS WEEK

For this TalkSheet discussion, you'll need a CD player and the Rich Mullins song "Where You Are" so you can play it for your group. You'll also want to provide a copy of the lyrics so your students can follow along. *(www.kidbrothers.net/wabairi1.html#wya)*

OPENER

Begin the conversation by talking about a time when you and your friends were in a dangerous situation. If you have a story from your high school years, it might help connect your life with your students' so they can relate to you even better. Your story will set up their first question.

THE DISCUSSION, BY NUMBERS

1. Turn the tables and let your group share their own dangerous experiences. Remember, it's important that their stories deal with a time they were with their friends.

2. Have your group complete the sentences on questions two and three before sharing them with the group.

3. See question two.

4. Before you play "Where You Are," let your group know that you'll be asking them to relate their lives to one of the three Bible stories mentioned in the song. After the song ends, take a few minutes to review the story of Daniel in the lions' den; Jonah in the belly of the fish; and Shadrach, Meshach, and Abednego in the blazing furnace. Choose a volunteer to retell them (be ready to fill in any gaps) or just offer your own condensed version of each story. Ask your students to share which Bible story relates to their own life experiences and why they chose it.

5. Give them an opportunity to share a current trial they're experiencing and when they're most likely to pray during the day. This question is meant to help you emphasize the importance of prayer on a daily basis. You may want to share your own crisis and the time of day that you set aside to pray as a model for them to consider.

6. Now have them turn to Romans 8:35-39, read the passage, and write down the one word or phrase that most accurately describes the way they feel about God today. Ask students to share their word or phrase with the group and why they chose it. Remind them of the promise of this passage and how closely it relates to the title of the song: "Where You Are." Nothing can separate us from God and his love. God is always where we are no matter how we feel or what we've done.

7. How might the truth of Romans 8:35-39 affect their approach to difficult situations like the one they described in question one? Let them share their answers with the group before moving on to the final question.

8. This last question will allow them to talk through what it looks like to "reach out" to God. Let them brainstorm and talk about how they might reach out to God right now in their lives.

THE CLOSE

Challenge your group to take a few minutes every day this week to pray, reach out to God, and review the three stories mentioned in the song. Close your time by having your students break off into smaller groups of two or three to pray about some of the trials they shared in question five.

MORE

• **Have your students compare Romans 8:35-39 with Psalm 139:5-16.**

• **Discuss how Jesus' words to his disciples in Matthew 28:18-20 relate to this discussion.**

• **Begin a character study on the life of Rich Mullins by asking for volunteers to read and discuss the book *Rich Mullins: An Arrow Pointing to Heaven* by James Bryan Smith.**

1. According to Genesis 2:24, what was God's original formula for couples to stay together?

GOD-MATH...
1 + 1 = 1

2. Read Genesis 2:18-25 and help your group to figure out...

• Why did God create "the couple" in the first place? (v. 18)

• What was deemed "suitable" for Adam? (v. 22)

• What does the Bible tell us about the state of this couple's relationship? (v. 25)

3. Genesis 3 unfolds the story of Adam and Eve: They disobeyed God and ate forbidden fruit from a tree that was off-limits. Read Genesis 3:7-10 and compare their reactions and feelings to how things were in Genesis 2:25.

4. What conclusions might you draw from the comparison in question three regarding who God desires you to be while in a relationship with someone of the opposite sex?

5. What insights regarding sexual intimacy did you have concerning the Scotch tape?

From *Still More High School TalkSheets: 50 Creative Discussions for Your Youth Group* by Dr. David W. Rogers. Permission to reproduce this page granted only for use in buyer's youth group. Copyright © 2009 by Youth Specialties. *www.youthspecialties.com*

THIS WEEK

This TalkSheet will show that God desires and designed sexual intimacy to occur within the marriage relationship between a man and a woman. God's math is One Man + One Woman = One Person united in body and spirit or 1 + 1 = 1.

OPENER

Ask your students to name some well-known celebrity couples (either married or dating) who are still together and some celebrity couples who aren't together anymore. Write their responses on a whiteboard. Then ask them to answer the first question on their Talk-Sheets.

THE DISCUSSION, BY NUMBERS

1. God's formula is One Man + One Woman = One Flesh (Person). Or 1 + 1 = 1. The words "one flesh" mean that two people of the opposite sex are to be sexually intimate with one another, as well as one in spirit. One flesh is meant to last "until death parts them." (See Matthew 19:5, Malachi 2:13-16, and Hebrews 13:4.)

2. Make sure the following observations are made before proceeding to the next question.
   - v. 18 tells us "It is not good for the man to be alone." Relationships were the intended design from the beginning.
   - v. 22 shows that God decided a woman was the most suitable helpmate for the man—not an animal or another man. Genesis 1:27 says, "Male and female he created them."
   - v. 25 indicates the man and woman were a couple and they were naked. However, because they were in a healthy, God-designed relationship, they felt no shame, no guilt, and no condemnation.

3. Set up the context of Genesis 3—Adam and Eve were naked, they had all they could eat, and they had the whole place to themselves. The one thing God commanded them *not* to do was eat from one tree. If they disobeyed, they'd die. The serpent entered the scene and led Adam and Eve to question God's boundaries. And they chose to eat the forbidden fruit. Verses 7-10 show how people react when they knowingly disobey God and suffer the consequences: They saw they were naked; they tried to cover themselves; and they hid because they'd deliberately disobeyed.

4. You want your group to make the following observation: As long as men and women are living within God's relational guidelines, there's no shame in who we are or what we're doing with a person of the opposite sex.

5. Ask for a male volunteer who'll let you put a piece of Scotch tape on his bare arm. Tell him you need to rip it off quickly. As you do, point out that every time two people have sex, it's as though the two are coming together in sexual "stickiness." God intended sex to be a bonding action between a man and a woman. However, when you "do it because it feels good" and then "do it" with another person, it's like sticking that used piece of tape onto another person's arm. (Stick the tape on someone else and rip it off again.) Now you have the hair and skin from two people on the tape. (This is a great time to bring up STDs.) If you keep using the tape over and over again, the tape looses its "stickiness." Sex was intended to be a bonding element between a man and a woman in the context of marriage. When people have sex outside of marriage, it loses its sacred meaning. (Stick a clean piece of tape to another clean piece.) That's the proper visual context for how 1 + 1 = 1. It's difficult to tell where one piece ends and the other begins.

CLOSE

Close by giving your students the opportunity to wrap a piece of Scotch tape around the ring finger on their left hand to signal their commitment to stay sexually pure. Close your time by praying for their sexual purity and commitment to live well in their relationships with members of the opposite sex.

MORE
- **Consider incorporating a True Love Waits commitment time. (See *www.lifeway.com/tlw/* for more information.)**
- **Have your students create accountability groups that form "purity pacts" as a way to keep each other accountable in their commitment to sexual purity.**
- **Consider inviting an adult who's received redemption from poor sexual choices to share her story. Such a testimony should give hope and encouragement to those who've already made poor sexual choices and need to see a living example of how God gives second chances.**

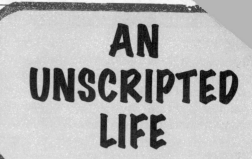

AN UNSCRIPTED LIFE

1. If you were to write a script of your life and it became a Hollywood movie, which actor would you cast to play you?

2. Since you can write anything you like into the story, how would the script of your life unfold?

3. Up to this point in your life, what are the best and worst unscripted moments you've experienced?

   • Best

   • Worst

4. Check out Job 1:20-21 and write what these verses mean in terms of your life's script.

5. Why do people usually feel it's okay for God to give but it's never okay for God to take away?

6. Read chapter one of Job and list the unscripted blessings God gave to Job.

7. From this same chapter, list the unscripted ways that God allowed Job's blessings to be taken away.

8. According to Job 1:20-22, how did Job respond to the unscripted parts of his story?

From *Still More High School TalkSheets: 50 Creative Discussions for Your Youth Group* by Dr. David W. Rogers. Permission to reproduce this page granted only for use in buyer's youth group. Copyright © 2009 by Youth Specialties. *www.youthspecialties.com*

of life is that there are many "unscripted"
Some are unscripted blessings, and others
ipted difficulties. During this discussion your
group will compare their life "scripts" with Job's response to some unscripted moments in his life.

OPENER

Start by asking your group to share their favorite movies and types of movies: Drama, romantic comedy, action, horror, and so on. Then share one of your favorites
that's well-written. Highlight the importance of a good
script. Before a movie is filmed, a script has to be written and the characters must be cast so the script can
come alive. Now ask your students to consider question one on the TalkSheet.

THE DISCUSSION, BY NUMBERS

1. Have some fun with this. Ask why they chose the ac-
tors they did, and then let the group decide whether
they agree or disagree with each student's choice.
2. Ask your group to think about how the script of
their lives would unfold from this moment forward.
Make sure they know there are no limits on the future. However, they can only write from this point
forward; they cannot change the past. After you give
them some time to think, let them share a synopsis
of their script. (The group doesn't get a say in this
part of the discussion.)
3. Now make the transition to what their current script
says. Have them reflect on the Best and the Worst unscripted moments in their life so far and share them
with the group. Be sensitive regarding their Worst
moments. If appropriate, you may want to stop and
pray for any struggling individuals.
4. You want your group to read Job 1:20-21, process
it, and internalize it to the degree that they can tell
you what it means in their own words. They could
write something like, "Good and bad stuff happens
in life; that's reality. Whatever happens, I'll choose to
praise God no matter what." Ask them to share their
answers with the group.
5. Sometimes it's good to let them sit with tough
questions. Don't feel like you have to bail them out
of the silence. See what they come up with. If nothing, then encourage them to think and pray about
it this week.

6. Have your group pair off and explore Job 1. They
should answer questions six and seven before sharing their findings with the group. Job's unscripted
blessings include seven sons and three daughters—
that's 10 children (a significant number indicating
special blessing in biblical days); 7,000 sheep; 3,000
camels; 500 yoke of oxen; 500 donkeys; and a large
number of servants. He was known as "the greatest man among all the people of the East" (in other
words, Job had a great reputation). Job enjoyed cel-
ebrating life with his children and their families (1:4).
7. All that was taken away in Job 1:13-19 were the
very things that were given to him as blessings in
Job 1:2-4.
8. Job's perspective is that God owes him nothing, yet
Job chooses to praise his Maker because God is wor-
thy of praise—regardless of Job's difficult situation.
Encourage your group to see the deeper meaning
behind the text and how it fits into their own lives.
9. Have your students share one of each and then ask
them to consider how it would honor God if they'd
choose to respond like Job in all things: "Blessed be
the name of the LORD" (v. 21, NKJV).

THE CLOSE

Allow your group to pray silently about how they've responded to life's unscripted moments and how they'll
respond in the future. As they pray, play the Matt Redman song that's based on this passage: "Blessed Be Your
Name." When the song ends, pray over your group and
dismiss them.

MORE

• While the Matt Redman song is playing, have your group
write letters of praise and response to God for both the
unscripted blessings and difficulties in their lives. The letter should be their written praise for who God is and what
God has done in their lives.
• Challenge your group to text BLESSED BE THE NAME OF
THE LORD to each other every day this week as a reminder that no matter what happens, they'll choose to bless
God's name.
• Explore how God can bring beauty out of the worst unscripted moments in our lives. Don't make light of their
situations. Rather, challenge them to view their difficult
situations from a new vantage point. There could be an
unscripted opportunity waiting for them.

1. List things that you really like.

2. List things that you really dislike.

3. When you think about "God's will for your life," is your first thought that you'll like it or dislike it? Why?

4. Read Psalm 139:13-18. How might these verses affect your answer to question three?

5. If God's will for your life is intended to taste good, then is it an acquired taste or does it naturally taste good to you? Why?

6. Now check out Psalm 37:4 and write it down. According to this verse, how do you see your tastes for the things you like and God's will for your life fitting together?

7. Read Romans 12:2 and jot it down. How are people supposed to be "transformed" by their minds?

8. What's the correlation in Romans 12:2 between what a person thinks and God's will for that person's life?

9. My best chance to know and experience God's will is to…

From *Still More High School TalkSheets: 50 Creative Discussions for Your Youth Group* by Dr. David W. Rogers. Permission to reproduce this page granted only for use in buyer's youth group. Copyright © 2009 by Youth Specialties. www.youthspecialties.com

THIS WEEK

This TalkSheet examines a premise that we can know God's will for our lives by understanding how God made us in terms of our likes and dislikes. It makes sense that the better we know ourselves as the created ones, the better we'll know our Creator.

OPENER

Create two lists of items on a whiteboard or large sheet of paper. Don't say what the categories are; just write things you like in one list and things you dislike in another. Ask your group if they can guess the significance of each list. Then have them look to questions one and two on their TalkSheets.

THE DISCUSSION, BY NUMBERS

1. Have your group answer questions one and two before sharing their lists. Take some time and let your students get to know each other better.

2. See question one.

3. Introduce the concept of "God's will for your lives" and how it might fit in with their likes and dislikes. Probe their answers without chiming in too much. This is an opinion question, so reassure them there's no right or wrong answer.

4. Now have someone read aloud Psalm 139:13-18. Help them reframe question three in light of what these verses say. Hopefully they'll mention how our creative Designer pays attention to all the details of our lives, including our likes and dislikes.

5. There are great cases to be made on both sides of this question, since addiction to sin has thrown our taste buds out of whack. However, let them grapple with this and form their own opinions.

6. At this point you want them to consider how their tastes can help them understand God's will for their lives. Note: Our tastes for the things we like will never violate what the Bible says about things that are good, holy, right, and true. If we have an attraction to something that's sinful, then it's certainly not God's will that we engage in it.

7. We're to renew our minds by replacing the thoughts of the world with the thoughts of God. A byproduct of this renewal process is that we can know the good, pleasing, and perfect (think "complete," rather than "without flaw") will of God for our lives. In part "renewing" our minds means we replace off-target thinking with a more accurate perspective. Doing this helps people discern between a healthy "good" taste and an unhealthy "good" taste. Sin tastes good. (If it didn't, then everyone would avoid it.) Thus, we must be careful we don't justify our sin by blaming God for creating us with an attraction to sin. That argument results in conforming to the world's philosophy of moral relativity.

8. If a person's mind is conformed to the views and principles of the world without being informed—and thus, *transformed*—by what God says in the Bible, then it'll be difficult for that person to know God's will for her life. If someone's mind is informed by what God says about life, then that person can filter what may or may not be God's will through God's perspective.

9. Their answers should include reading the Bible, praying, listening to the wisdom of mature followers of Jesus, drawing from their life experiences, and paying attention to their circumstances as well as their likes and dislikes. Remember, a person will never be in the will of God if she's doing something that God has spoken against in the Bible. However, if God doesn't speak to a particular issue, then she should feel free to go with her preference. God allows some gray areas in which we can choose whatever we like.

THE CLOSE

Challenge your students to create a running list of things they like and dislike so they can add to it over the coming weeks, months—even years. Every time they add something, they should ask God to continue using their likes and dislikes to reveal God's will. One of the greatest ways we can know God's will for our lives is to know ourselves.

MORE

- **Ask how people are supposed to "take delight in the LORD" as Psalm 37:4 encourages us to do.**
- **Discuss what they currently understand God's will for their lives to be.**
- **Have your group discuss people who live according to God's will. What characteristics do they exhibit? How did they arrive at doing God's will? Do they seem to enjoy life?**

1. If you wanted to find out what's going on around the world, what news sources would you most likely turn to for this information?

EXTRA, EXTRA! READ ALL ABOUT IT!

2. How informed are you about what's going on around the world? Rate yourself on a scale of 1 to 10 (with 1 being not very informed and 10 being extremely informed) and give reasons for your answer.

3. "Read the Bible in one hand and your newspaper in the other." What do you think this quotation means?

4. "We are to be in the world but not of the world." What do you think this quotation means?

5. How do you think the quotes from questions three and four might inform your understanding of the following Bible verses?

   • 1 Chronicles 12:32

   • Daniel 1:1-4, 17-20

   • Acts 17:16-34 (especially v. 28)

6. How might knowing what's happening in our world benefit you in being who God desires for you to be and what God wants you to be about?

7. What steps do you need to take if you're to be known as those in 1 Chronicles 12:32 were known—people who "understood the times and knew what Israel should do"?

From *Still More High School TalkSheets: 50 Creative Discussions for Your Youth Group* by Dr. David W. Rogers. Permission to reproduce this page granted only for use in buyer's youth group. Copyright © 2009 by Youth Specialties. www.youthspecialties.com

THIS WEEK

This TalkSheet will demonstrate the importance of knowing what's going on in the world so we might influence the world for Christ. God uses people to engage the world so they can change the world. But it's difficult to impact a world we know little or nothing about.

OPENER

Ask your students to list their favorite Web sites or the sites they go to the most and why they like them. If you can bring up these sites on a computer as they're listing them, then it's likely to get them more engaged in the discussion.

THE DISCUSSION, BY NUMBERS

1. These could be other Web sites, TV stations, magazines, well-informed people, or the newspaper. Feel free to share the resources you use, if necessary.

2. Have your group rate themselves as to how informed they are about current affairs and world events. Do they believe it's important to be informed? Why or why not?

3. Too often, Christians pay attention to the Bible at the exclusion of the world. But knowing what's happening around them will help Christians (a) know how to share God's love, (b) know where evil and injustice are thriving, (c) know how to pray for God to change lives, and so on.

4. Christians are to be people set apart (different) by the way they live, love, serve, and share with others. However, God never intended for his followers to sequester themselves into holy huddles. It's hard to share Christ and demonstrate the gospel if we never spend time with the people who need to hear and experience the love of Christ. We're to be a people of conviction and compassion.

5. These passages illustrate how devoted followers of God used their knowledge of the world to impact and influence others for Christ.
   - 1 Chronicles 12:32—men from the tribe of Issachar "understood the times" and knew what Israel should do in battle. We must also be a people who know what's going on so we can do what God desires in our communities.
   - Daniel 1:1-4, 17-20—even in exile, God allowed Shadrach, Meshach, Abednego, and Daniel to receive an education and master the subjects of

study in a pagan society. In a sense, they were missionaries who diligently learned the language and culture so they could not only navigate it, but also influence others in the ways of the one true God.
   - Acts 17:16-34—This example shows that not only did Paul know the teachings of Jesus, but he'd also read and could easily work into conversation the poets and philosophers of other cultures. Paul was a master at meeting people where they were at and taking the conversation to a place that engaged the gospel.

6. When followers of Jesus demonstrate that they're engaged and up-to-speed with what's going on in the world, nonbelievers may be more open to hearing about the things of God that inform our lives. But when we're viewed as "odd for God" and being "out of touch" with the real world, it's hard to have legitimate conversations with people that might lead to friendships and ultimately life-changing decisions.

7. Suggest they take five minutes each day to read through the headlines of a newspaper—just to be aware of what's making the news—or access the various news Web sites from around the world.

THE CLOSE

Walk your group through the newspaper and let them choose both local and national headlines to pray about. They should view the paper with prayerful eyes before taking a few minutes to read the article they've chosen and pray about it.

MORE
- **Create a current events quiz from stories in today's paper. Divide your group into teams and ask them questions about some of the stories that made the headlines.**
- **Challenge your group to let the newspaper inform their prayer life. Encourage them to take five minutes each day to scan the headlines of the paper and then spend another five minutes praying about the things that are happening around the world.**
- **Select a place that's been in the news recently and challenge your group to specifically pray for that country in the coming week. Suggest they go online and find out as much as they can about that country. Challenge them to find places where God is at work and other places where God needs to work through the lives of believers. Discuss their findings next week.**

THEME SONGS

1. The theme song for my friends is…

2. The theme song for my relationship with my parents is…

3. The theme song of my parents is…

4. The theme song of my relationship with my family is…

5. The theme song of my teachers is…

6. The theme song of my whole life is…

7. What does David say the theme song of his life revolves around in Psalm 119:54?

8. Why do you think David made this the theme of his song?

9. What do you think the theme song of Jesus' life is?

10. If Jesus were to give you a new theme song for your life today, what do you think it would be and why?

From *Still More High School TalkSheets: 50 Creative Discussions for Your Youth Group* by Dr. David W. Rogers. Permission to reproduce this page granted only for use in buyer's youth group. Copyright © 2009 by Youth Specialties. www.youthspecialties.com

THIS WEEK
Today you'll let the music guide the conversation as your students determine their theme songs for various relationships and then compare their songs to the theme of David's song found in Psalm 119:54.

OPENER
Create a playlist of your favorite songs to represent the theme songs of your life. Use the questions on the TalkSheet to get started. Have your theme songs playing when your group enters the room. (You'll also need to ask your students to bring their portable music players to the meeting.) Start by telling your group that the songs they hear are some of the theme songs for your life. Then give them 5 to 10 minutes to answer questions one through six on their TalkSheets. Make sure their answers include a reason as to why that particular song was chosen. For each question, let all of the students take turns playing the first few seconds of their theme song (via an iPod dock or computer speakers) so the rest of the group can hear and try to guess the name of the song. If you don't have time to do this for everyone, then just do it for question six.

THE DISCUSSION, BY NUMBERS
1. The theme song for your friends should be an indicator of their values, their philosophy of life, and the things they're interested in. You may want to describe it as, "This is the song that would play when your friends walk into the room."
2. This song could be funny or show great insight into what's going on at home. Be sensitive as you talk with your students about their song choices.
3. Have some fun with the theme song for their parents.
4. This theme song should extend beyond the parents to include siblings and grandparents and so on. Be wise in your comments and take mental notes on how you might be able to pray for your students in their family relationships.
5. Let them take some shots at their teachers in a fun way, but make sure it doesn't get out of hand.
6. This one's tricky. They'll have to boil down all of their song selections into one theme song for their whole life. If your group knows each other well,

let the group designate what each other's theme song should be. This could be both insightful and affirming, if done in the right spirit. It could also be hurtful if done in a teasing manner. Make sure you set the right tone.

7. Now have your group write out Psalm 119:54 and answer the question. (God's decrees)
8. Ask a few probing questions concerning the definition of *decree* and what they know about David's life. Basically, David is saying he's basing his whole life around the things God said to do—no matter where he is in life. For David it's not just a Sunday thing.
9. Let them run with this one a bit. Ask them to talk about the events and characteristics in Jesus' life that should be considered in determining his theme song. If they need some help getting started, mention all-knowing, gentle, truthful, full of grace, and authority, as well as healing people, rising from the dead, feeding people, and being focused on his mission.
10. Wrap up your time by talking about the theme song Jesus would like to give them based on his dreams and desires for their lives.

THE CLOSE
Choose a song that you'd like your group to think about as it pertains to their lives. Print the lyrics and pass out copies to the group so they can see what's being sung over them while they listen. Choose a song that's meaningful and speaks truth into their lives. Consider songs from David Crowder Band, Robbie Seay Band, Chris Tomlin, or Rita Springer.

MORE
• **Personalize your songs for your students by giving them a suggestion to download. Let them know you've prayed those lyrics over their lives.**
• **Play "Name That Tune" to spice up the discussion and add a little competition. Do this at the beginning of your time as you play the theme songs to your own life.**
• **Feel free to ditch the iPods and MP3 players component and go straight to discussion if you're worried about some students not having portable music devices. Most teens would be able to work through the discussion without hearing the music or referencing their iPods to answer the questions.**

1. My favorite time of day is _____ _____ because…

2. My least favorite time of day is _____ _____ because…

3. My favorite time of the week is _____ _____ because…

WHAT TIME IS IT?

4. My least favorite time of the week is _____ because…

5. My favorite time of year is _____ because…

6. My least favorite time of year is _____ because…

7. Check out Ecclesiastes 3:1-11. What are these verses saying about time?

8. List three things for which the timing is right in your life.

9. List three things for which the timing isn't right in your life (but you wish it were).

10. Read verse 11 again. Would you describe this time in your life as "beautiful," or would you choose a different word? What word and why?

11. Describe a time when God did something beautiful in your life.

12. The thing in my life that I need God to make beautiful is…

From *Still More High School TalkSheets: 50 Creative Discussions for Your Youth Group* by Dr. David W. Rogers. Permission to reproduce this page granted only for use in buyer's youth group. Copyright © 2009 by Youth Specialties. *www.youthspecialties.com*

THIS WEEK

This week your group will look at a passage that talks about there being a right time for everything and how God makes everything beautiful in its time. *Beautiful* may not be the best word to describe the teenage years, so this promise is one they should hold on to.

OPENER

Set up a big clock to help your group remember the discussion. Start by asking what time their alarm goes off in the morning or when they get out of bed. Then have them complete questions one through six on their TalkSheets.

THE DISCUSSION, BY NUMBERS

1. The first six questions will get your students talking about their favorite and least favorite times of the day, week, and year. Have the students take turns sharing and explaining their responses.

2. See question one.

3. See question one.

4. See question one.

5. See question one.

6. See question one.

7. Ask a volunteer to read Ecclesiastes 3:1-11 out loud. Give the students a moment to answer; then have them share their responses. Hopefully someone will say these verses speak about the various seasons in a person's life and how God makes all things beautiful.

8. Split the group into teams and have them answer questions eight and nine together. You may need to offer a few examples to get them started, such as studying hard, dating with boundaries, and honoring your parents.

9. See question eight. Some examples might be sexual intimacy, making money, and becoming more involved in politics.

10. Have someone reread Ecclesiastes 3:11. If they could use only one word to describe their life, what would it be? Would it be the word *beautiful* or another word? Have them explain their answers.

11. Ask your group to share about a time when God did something beautiful in their lives. Offer an example to help set the tone.

12. This final question could be a painful one. Encourage your group to be vulnerable and honest with one another. Take notes on what your group is sharing and consider some specific ways you could encourage them in the coming days. If the students are hesitant to share, set the tone by giving your answer first.

CLOSE

Wrap up your time by praying that God would make your students' lives beautiful in time.

MORE

• Challenge your group to set aside a specific time each day to pray for those students who are still waiting for God to make a difficult situation beautiful (question 12).

• Encourage your students to text each other the phrase BEAUTIFUL IN TIME at different times throughout the week.

• As a group spend time serving others and making their lives beautiful in a tangible way: Plant flowers in someone's garden, clean up a public park, or paint over graffiti.

1. What gear are you in with your friends?

2. What gear are you in with your parents?

3. What gear are you in with your image?

4. What gear are you in with your schoolwork?

WHAT GEAR ARE YOU IN?

5. What gear are you in with your extracurricular activities?

6. What gear are you in with your commitments?

7. What gear are you in with your convictions about what's right and wrong?

8. What gear are you in when it comes to your relationship with Jesus?

9. Check out John 8:1-11. What gear do you think these people were in?
   - The teachers of the law and the Pharisees

   - The woman caught in adultery

   - Jesus

10. What's the significance of Jesus' words to the woman in verse 11? What gear did he desire for her to be in?

11. What do these two statements mean to you as they pertain to the John 8 story and the gear our lives are in?
   - "God did not create you to live in neutral."

   - "God did not free you to live in reverse."

12. What do you need to do to begin shifting gears in your life with Jesus?

From *Still More High School TalkSheets: 50 Creative Discussions for Your Youth Group* by Dr. David W. Rogers. Permission to reproduce this page granted only for use in buyer's youth group. Copyright © 2009 by Youth Specialties. www.youthspecialties.com

THIS WEEK

Your group will evaluate the health of their relationships by comparing them to the gears of an automobile. Because so many people begin driving during high school, this should be a lot of fun as they consider which direction they're headed within their various relationships and commitments.

OPENER

Start by asking your students to share their stories about learning how to drive. How are their parents handling this new adventure? Now shift the conversation toward one aspect of driving—putting the car in gear. Have them name as many gears as they can and give a general description of each. As they do, write the names of the gears on a whiteboard or large piece of paper. Some examples might be—

- First gear = starts off slow and has good pulling power
- Second gear = increasing speed that leads to a higher and faster gear
- Third through sixth gears = increasing speed that eventually leads to the fastest pace (overdrive)
- Overdrive = the final or "top" gear; normally used for cruising down the highway
- Four-wheel drive = used for off-road adventures and in situations with low traction (ice, loose gravel, and so on)
- Reverse = sends the vehicle backward
- Neutral = allows the vehicle to keep running without going in any direction

Once they're familiar with the various gears, have them answer questions one through eight on their Talk-Sheets.

THE DISCUSSION, BY NUMBERS

1. Give everyone a chance to share their answer and why they chose that particular gear before moving on to the next question.
2. See question one.
3. See question one.
4. See question one.
5. See question one.
6. See question one.
7. See question one.
8. See question one.
9. Ask someone to read John 8:1-11. Then have your students pair off and answer this question together before sharing their responses with the group. Point out that the people in the story may use more than one "gear." For instance, the teachers of the law and the Pharisees come barreling into the temple in four-wheel drive, towing the accused woman behind them. After they unhitch her before Jesus, they're waiting in neutral, revving their engines and preparing to slam it into drive and peel out—right over the top of her.
10. Have your group focus on verse 11. When Jesus tells the woman, "Go now and leave your life of sin," he's telling her to put her life into first gear and begin moving forward again. She's been pulled out of the ditch of adultery, and she's ready to drive on. Process this idea with your group and ask what gear she might be moving toward during this part of the conversation.
11. Your students should jot down their responses to both quotes before discussing them as a group, one quote at a time. The first quote deals with being paralyzed by sin and never moving forward in life because of fear, guilt, or the unknown. The second quote deals with freedom in Christ—like what the woman in John 8 experienced. Too often we get a mixed taste for sin and grace. We like the taste of both, so we never flee the sin and live in the light of God's grace. Jesus intends for his followers to move forward in freedom, rather than repeatedly reversing their lives into the ditch of sin.
12. Let your group finish the discussion by applying what they've learned to their own lives. Let them share their thoughts and ideas with the group.

THE CLOSE

Pass out Matchbox cars to remind your students to move forward at a healthy pace and to maintain control as they shift gears in their relationships this week. The car should remind them to pray often about the appropriate gear for their relationships.

MORE

- Take your group to a parking lot and see which licensed students can parallel park the best.
- *The Wonder Years* has a great episode called "Road Test" (from the Season Five DVD). Kevin is trying to get his driver's permit, and he can't parallel park. He sneaks out of the house to practice one night and winds up running over the lawn mower. Watch this episode as a group before discussing the TalkSheet.
- Teach your group how to drive a stick shift!

1. List three things that typically disturb people.

2. What's one thing you do that seems to disturb your parents?

3. What's one thing your parents do that disturbs you?

PLEASE, DO DISTURB

4. Describe a time in your life when you were really disturbed.

5. Check out Isaiah 6:1-7. What disturbed Isaiah and why?

6. What's one thing in life that really disturbs you that you think also probably disturbs God?

7. Read Isaiah 29:13-14. What disturbed God in these verses and why?

8. If there was one thing in my life that was disturbing God today, it would probably be…

9. If I could do one thing that would ease the heart of God, I think it would be…

10. What would happen if you asked God to disturb you with the things in life that disturb him?

Disturb us, Lord, when
We are too pleased with ourselves,
When our dreams have come true
Because we dreamed too little,
When we arrived safely
Because we sailed too close to the shore.

Disturb us, Lord, when
with the abundance of things we possess
We have lost our thirst
For the waters of life;
Having fallen in love with life,
We have ceased to dream of eternity
And in our efforts to build a new earth,

We have allowed our vision
Of the new Heaven to dim.
Disturb us, Lord, to dare more boldly,
To venture on wilder seas
Where storms will show Your mastery;
Where losing sight of land,
We shall find the stars.
We ask you to push back
The horizons of our hopes;
And to push back the future
In strength, courage, hope, and love.
This we ask in the name of our Captain,
Who is Jesus Christ.

— Sir Francis Drake (1540–1596)

From *Still More High School TalkSheets: 50 Creative Discussions for Your Youth Group* by Dr. David W. Rogers. Permission to reproduce this page granted only for use in buyer's youth group. Copyright © 2009 by Youth Specialties. www.youthspecialties.com

THIS WEEK

It's disturbing when the lack of holiness of our lives comes face to face with the pure holiness of God. This TalkSheet will cover the subject of being "disturbed." What would happen if the things that disturb God also disturbed us? What if we asked God to "disturb us"?

OPENER

Start the discussion with an object lesson. Show your students a "Please, Do Not Disturb" door hanger like the ones found in most hotels. Talk about the significance of this sign and how it allows a person to get some sleep and not be disturbed by housecleaning personnel or others who want to enter the hotel room. Feel free to share any funny stories you might have about hotel stays or solicit some from your group. Then make the point that nobody puts out a "Please, Do Disturb" sign on their door. Head to the discussion questions and let them start talking about things in life that disturb them.

THE DISCUSSION, BY NUMBERS

1. Share a few examples of things that disturb you to get started. Then give your group a few minutes to come up with their top three things that disturb them.
2. Ask your group to answer questions two and three before sharing their responses with the group. Go over everyone's responses to question two before moving on to question three.
3. See question two.
4. Encourage them to think about a time when they were truly disturbed about something. Maybe it was the death of a family member or friend. Lead off and give an example from your own life to set the pace. Be mindful that this question could lead some students to share painful things. If appropriate, take time to pray as a group.
5. Have them read Isaiah 6:1-7 and talk about the things that disturbed Isaiah when he saw God. Then ask why those things disturbed him. Basically, Isaiah saw the holiness of God and then clearly saw his own sinfulness by comparison.

6. The goal of this question is to help your group feel connected to God. They might talk about things like injustice, poverty, or specific sins such as abuse or abandonment. Give your group a bit of time on this one and see what they come up with before moving on to the next question.
7. Now have your group read Isaiah 29:13-14 to see what things disturb God. These verses suggest that God is disturbed by lives that don't authenticate our words. God doesn't like hypocrisy—inauthentic lives that proclaim one thing but do another. Perhaps your students are a lot like God in this area.
8. Have your group take a few minutes to think about and answer these last three questions. Let each student answer all three questions before the next person answers.
9. See question eight.
10. See question eight.

THE CLOSE

End your time by asking your group to silently read through the prayer at the bottom of their Talk-Sheets. It's a prayer that Sir Francis Drake prayed in 1577. Then pray it out loud in unison to close your time.

MORE

• Give each student a "Please, Do Not Disturb" door hanger and have them cross out the word not as a reminder of the discussion. Challenge them to hang it in a place where they'll see it each day.

• Challenge your group to pray Sir Francis Drake's prayer every day this week.

• Show clips from the MTV show *Scarred*, a show about disturbing images and the wounds people have received while doing extreme sports. (Caution: Sometimes the images are very disturbing. Preview the show ahead of time and make wise decisions about any content that may not be appropriate for your group.)

1. My parents constantly remind me to…

2. I never need to be reminded about…

3. I always need to be reminded about…

4. Whether I want to admit it or not, I have a hard time remembering to…

5. I constantly have to remind _____
   about _____.

6. _____ constantly has to remind me
   about _____.

7. My generation needs to be reminded about…

8. My generation doesn't need to be reminded about…

9. My parents' generation needs to be reminded about…

10. My parents' generation doesn't need to be reminded about…

11. I wish someone would remind my friends to…

12. I wish someone would remind _____ about _____.

13. "People need to be reminded more than they need to be instructed." What do you think this quote by Samuel Johnson really means?

14. Check out 1 Corinthians 11:23-29. What does that passage say we need to remember?

15. Why do you believe it's so important to remember those things?

16. What do verses 27-29 say will be the consequences for a person who doesn't remember these things?

17. Why do you think that's such a big deal?

18. How might my approach to the day be different if I took a few moments each morning to think about these things and truly remember what verses 23-26 are all about?

JUST A REMINDER

From *Still More High School TalkSheets: 50 Creative Discussions for Your Youth Group* by Dr. David W. Rogers. Permission to reproduce this page granted only for use in buyer's youth group. Copyright © 2009 by Youth Specialties. www.youthspecialties.com

20. JUST A REMINDER—Remembering the meaning behind the Lord's Supper
(1 Corinthians 11:23-29)

THIS WEEK
This TalkSheet focuses on the significance of remembering the true meaning of the Lord's Supper. Jesus tells his followers to "do this in remembrance of me." What would a follower of Jesus' life look like if that person took time each day to be reminded of Jesus' sacrifice?

OPENER
Begin by tying a piece of string around your pointer finger and asking the group what it means. This used to be a simple way for people to remind themselves of something they had to do. Show a clip from *It's a Wonderful Life* in which Uncle Billy (played by Thomas Mitchell) has a string on his finger to remind him to take the deposit to the bank. Ask your group to share other ways they remind themselves of things they have to do, such as making a list, sticking a note on the refrigerator or mirror, and so on. After you finish this part of your discussion, move to the TalkSheet and have your group answer the first 12 questions before pausing to share them with the rest of the group.

THE DISCUSSION, BY NUMBERS
1. Your students should complete the sentences in the first 12 questions dealing with reminders. Afterward, take time to let them share their answers before moving forward with question 13.
2. See question one.
3. See question one.
4. See question one.
5. See question one.
6. See question one.
7. See question one.
8. See question one.
9. See question one.
10. See question one.
11. See question one.
12. See question one.
13. Let your group talk through their understanding of the following quote by Samuel Johnson: "People need to be reminded more than they need to be instructed." Do they agree or disagree? Why?
14. Have your group read 1 Corinthians 11:23-29. Paul says it's important not to take the Lord's Supper lightly. Rather, followers of Jesus are to remember the true meaning of this holy act of worship. Jesus instructed his disciples to take time to "remember" the significance of the bread and the cup. Let your group talk through these things as they read the passage together.

15. Beyond the fact that Jesus told us to "do this in remembrance of him," for what other reasons should followers of Jesus take time to be reminded of the significance of Jesus' sacrifice when participating in Communion?
16. Verses 27-29 indicate that people who take Communion in a thoughtless or routine (unworthy) manner will eat and drink judgment on themselves.
17. Let your group members wrestle with this question before sharing your own insights. Regardless of whether or not we fully understand the meaning of these warnings, it's clear that people are to approach the Lord's Supper with reverence and in a manner that humbly and fully deals with any sin in their lives before eating or drinking. In other words, get right with God before remembering him in the act of Communion.
18. Wrap up your discussion by letting your group consider how their days might be different if they started each one by taking time to remember the significance of Jesus' sacrifice.

THE CLOSE
Take a few moments to let your group write a note of prayer to Jesus. In it, encourage them to confess sin, examine their lives, and thank Jesus for the sacrifice he made on the cross. Challenge them to begin their note of prayer with this statement: "Jesus, today I'm reminded of…." Then let them conclude their time by taking Communion as a group. Be sure to talk with your pastor or other church leaders about the logistics of serving the Lord's Supper to your students so you respect the tradition of your church.

MORE
• **Challenge your students to start each day by eating a piece of toast and drinking a glass of grape juice to remind themselves of Jesus' sacrifice. Thus, breakfast just became a reminder of the great love that Jesus has for people.**
• **Suggest that your students text the word REMEMBER to others in the group this week to remind them of Jesus' sacrifice.**
• **Challenge your group to wear a string on their finger this week to remind them to live for Jesus. When people ask them what the string is for, encourage them to share their faith with them.**

1. List three areas of your life that you feel are sufficiently "hydrated."

2. List three areas of your life that you feel are cramping up and in need of an IV.

3. My soul feels hydrated and fully alive when…

4. My soul feels dry and thirsty when…

5. The things dripping into my life right now are…

6. If I could have one thing *stop* dripping into my life, it would be…

7. If I could have one thing *begin* dripping into my life, it would be…

8. What do you think John 7:37-39 has to do with your soul IV?

9. How would someone "hook up" her soul to such a drip?

10. What's the biggest reason people don't stay hooked up to such a drip?

11. How would your soul and life respond if you began a John 7:37 drip?

SOUL IV

From *Still More High School TalkSheets: 50 Creative Discussions for Your Youth Group* by Dr. David W. Rogers. Permission to reproduce this page granted only for use in buyer's youth group. Copyright © 2009 by Youth Specialties. *www.youthspecialties.com*

THIS WEEK

This TalkSheet uses the object lesson of a hospital IV to generate discussion. What would it look like if our souls were hooked up to intravenous fluids? What things are currently "dripping" into our souls? Are our souls dehydrated ("cramping") or fully hydrated?

OPENER

Start by displaying an IV bag from a local hospital. Generate discussion by asking your group to explain what an IV is used for and how it works. Basically, an IV is used to "feed" fluids or medicine from a "drip bag" that's connected by a tube to a hypodermic needle. The needle is inserted into a vein in a person's hand or arm, and a doctor regulates the rate of the drip. Often an IV is used to hydrate someone. Let your group have a few minutes to discuss how an IV works and when it's used before moving ahead to the questions on the TalkSheet. Leave them thinking about the concept of hydration as one of the primary uses of the IV and how oftentimes a person's body will "cramp" when it's dehydrated.

THE DISCUSSION, BY NUMBERS

1. Ask your group to think about their lives and list three areas in which they feel fully "hydrated" (in other words, healthy and in right standing with others). Perhaps a person is fully hydrated in their relationships with their friends, with their schoolwork, or with their dating relationships.
2. Now have your group consider three areas of their lives in which they feel as though they're cramping a bit. Examples might be their relationship with their parents, understanding their identity, or feeling accepted by friends.
3. Direct your group to answer questions three and four together before sharing their responses with everyone.
4. See question three.
5. Refer back to the tubing on the IV and ask the group to think about what's "dripping" into their lives and souls. Don't offer any examples. Simply encourage them to think about the things in their lives that are influencing them. These can be both healthy and unhealthy things.
6. Let your group answer questions six and seven together. Have them complete each sentence and then share their responses with the group.

7. See question six.
8. Have your group read John 7:37-39 and offer their thoughts. Basically, Jesus claims to be the source of soul hydration in this passage.
9. Challenge them to think through ways people might "hook up" their souls to a "Jesus drip" and then maintain the connection so their souls stay hydrated. Don't feel pressured to give your group the answer. Part of spiritual development and maturity involves wrestling with your own questions.
10. Have your group talk about various reasons why people don't stay "hydrated" with Jesus. Be a facilitator at this point. Note their answers and then have them think about solutions for these hindrances to soul hydration in Christ.
11. Challenge your group to dream a bit on this final question. What would their lives look like if they were constantly "hooked up" to Jesus? What does a fully hydrated soul look like?

THE CLOSE

Challenge your group to take the "hydration challenge" this week. It's recommended that a person drink eight glasses of water a day to stay fully hydrated. So challenge your group to pray and intentionally reconnect with Jesus eight times a day (while drinking a glass of water). See if a few students will commit to doing this for one week, and then have them share their experiences the following week. Ask them if their soul feels more or less hydrated after taking the challenge.

MORE

• **Invite a doctor or nurse to open the session by talking about how IVs are used and the effects of dehydration.**
• **To help make the point about thirsty and dry souls, show a clip from ¡Three Amigos! Dusty Bottoms, Lucky Day, and Ned Nederlander (played by Chevy Chase, Steve Martin, and Martin Short, respectively) are traveling across the desert, and Ned and Lucky look so thirsty. Then Dusty takes a huge drink from his canteen before throwing the remaining water on the ground and applying lip balm.**
• **Give everyone a glass of water to sip during this discussion as a way to tangibly taste the hydration.**

INGREDIENTS

1. What ingredients in your life tasted sweet?

2. What ingredients in your life tasted sour?

3. What ingredients in your life tasted good at first, but then left a bitter taste in your mouth?

4. What ingredients in your life were hard to swallow?

5. What ingredients in your life would you love to taste again?

6. What ingredients in your life do you pray you never have to taste again?

7. What ingredients do you hope to taste in your life someday?

8. What ingredients do you hope you never have to taste in your life someday?

9. Read Romans 8:28. What does this verse have to say concerning all the different ingredients of your life?

10. Today, I think my life tastes…

From *Still More High School TalkSheets: 50 Creative Discussions for Your Youth Group* by Dr. David W. Rogers. Permission to reproduce this page granted only for use in buyer's youth group. Copyright © 2009 by Youth Specialties. *www.youthspecialties.com*

22. INGREDIENTS—Viewing the elements of your life as ingredients that God desires to mix together to make something that "tastes good" (Romans 8:28)

THIS WEEK

Life is made up of both "difficult tasting" experiences as well as "tasty" experiences. However, when all of life's ingredients are mixed together and baked by God, something good is sure to be the end result.

OPENER

Start by having the ingredients for a cake laid out before your group. Talk about each ingredient that goes into a cake and then separate them into two areas on the table: Those that taste good on their own and those that don't taste good on their own. Talk about how it's not until all the ingredients are mixed together and baked at the appropriate temperature that the cake tastes the way it should. Use the cake and ingredients as a metaphor for the lives of your students. Then let them begin to work through the TalkSheet questions and talk about the various "ingredients" that make up their lives.

THE DISCUSSION, BY NUMBERS

1. Give your students a few minutes to work through questions one through eight before discussing their answers. You may want to give an example or two from your own life before turning them loose to think through the various "ingredients" of their lives. After they've had sufficient time to think, let them share their answers. It might be most effective to let all students answer the first question in full before moving on to the next question. Be sensitive to any responses that may elicit emotions from individuals in your group. If you feel it's appropriate, take time to stop and pray for those who share very vulnerable or difficult "ingredients."

2. See question one.
3. See question one.
4. See question one.
5. See question one.
6. See question one.
7. See question one.
8. See question one.
9. Have your group read Romans 8:28 and discuss the implications of that verse when compared to the metaphor of life as a baked cake. Talk about the hope this offers people that God will take all of the ingredients of our lives and use them to work "for the good of those who love him and have been called according to his purpose."
10. Let your group finish the statement concerning how they think their lives taste right now. Ask them to explain why they each chose that word. Then ask what would make their lives taste as good as they possibly could in the mouth of God.

THE CLOSE

End by serving cake to your group. Let them eat their cake as they share prayer requests with one another. Close the time by praying for each other.

MORE

• Divide your group into teams and have them bake cakes together at the home of one of their team members. While they bake their cake, have them talk through the various "ingredients" that make up their lives. How might God make something that "tastes good" out of so many different ingredients?

• Bake cakes as a group and then take them to widows or elderly people in your church or community as an act of love.

• Have a cake-eating contest to add a little humor and competition to the group.

1. List your top 10 champions of all time.

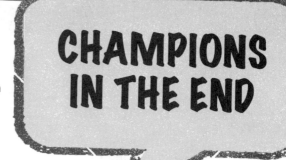

CHAMPIONS IN THE END

2. What are the characteristics or qualifications of a person or team that's considered a "champion"?

3. Have you ever been part of a championship team or earned the honor of being a champion? What kind of responses and rewards do champions typically receive for their achievements?

4. What thoughts come to your mind when you consider this statement: "Those who stay will be champions."

5. What do the following verses have to do with being a champion and sticking with something until the end?

   • Psalm 119:33

   • Psalm 119:111-112

   • John 13:1

6. How do you think the quote from question four pertains to the life of Jesus?

7. What things do you need to do to be considered a "champion" at the end of your life?

From *Still More High School TalkSheets: 50 Creative Discussions for Your Youth Group* by Dr. David W. Rogers. Permission to reproduce this page granted only for use in buyer's youth group. Copyright © 2009 by Youth Specialties. www.youthspecialties.com

23. CHAMPIONS IN THE END—Choosing to be a champion *(Psalm 119:33, 111-112; John 13:1; Philippians 2:5-11)*

THIS WEEK
This discussion revolves around the concept of being a champion and the choices they must make in order to be crowned a champion in the end.

OPENER
Begin by playing a word association game. Ask your students what comes to mind when you say the word *champion*. Can they name a few? Ask them to name champions in various arenas, such as basketball, football, baseball, soccer, golf, school, music, war, art, cooking, politics, and so on. Then ask them to take a look at the first question on the TalkSheet to begin the discussion.

THE DISCUSSION, BY NUMBERS
1. Have each person make a list of 10 champions who they believe should be recognized as the top 10 champions of all time.
2. Talk through the characteristics and qualifications of a champion, such as being disciplined, driven, and focused. Which of these could be identified in the lives of the people on their list in question one?
3. Have your group discuss how champions are treated. They're revered, honored, famous, and so on. If no one in your group has ever been a champion, have them imagine what it would be like and share their ideas with the group.
4. The late Bo Schembechler (former football coach for the University of Michigan) was known for making fiery speeches to his team. One time when his players were on the verge of giving up on the school's football program, Schembechler said: "Those who stay will be champions." The team was at a crisis of belief and had to decide whether or not to choose to do the hard work to overcome adversity.
5. The Psalmist considered knowing and following God's decrees as being of utmost importance. He wanted to be known as a man who lived by the things God valued in his Word. Making God happy by the way he lives his life will make him a champion in God's eyes. Choosing not to waver from this goal will also make him a champion because it blesses the heart of God. In the John passage, we see how Jesus loves his followers and friends to the very end. Regardless of their insuf-ficiencies and questions, the heart of Jesus—the Champion of the world—was full of deep love for people.
6. Challenge your group to think a bit deeper. What comes to their minds when they think about why Jesus came to earth? Hopefully they'll talk about Jesus staying focused on his mission despite the pain of the cross. Jesus didn't waver in his purity. He put all of his reward, honor, and heavenly joy aside in order to come to earth to be our Champion. Now have them read Philippians 2:5-11. Jesus set aside all of his glory to live as a man who would humble himself and die on a cross to gain all of humanity as his own. In the end, God raised him up and glorified him with the highest honor.
7. People don't stumble into being champions. It's something that's pursued with dogged devotion and discipline. Have your group talk about how their lives might need to be refocused and what needs to happen—starting today—if they desire to be a champion at the end of their lives.

THE CLOSE
Ask your group to commit to pray about one area of their lives that they'll incorporate as a discipline to move them closer to becoming a champion. Encourage them to share one thing that God brings to mind as they're praying, and then ask someone to hold them accountable as they incorporate this new discipline into their daily lives. Perhaps it's praying daily or studying more. Whatever it is, encourage them to begin taking steps toward becoming the person God desires them to be at the end of their lives.

MORE
• Play "We Are the Champions" by Queen as your group is coming and going.
• Show the animated "Crazy Frog—We Are the Champions (Ding a Dang Dong)" video on YouTube *(at www.youtube.com/watch?v=YCj-RyKCmHQ)* as an easy way to introduce the topic of "champions."
• If you have students or staff who are good at editing videos, ask them to create a montage of great champions from famous movie clips, such as *Rocky*, Maximus from *Gladiator*, Daniel-san from *The Karate Kid*, Jimmy Chitwood from *Hoosiers*, or even modern-day champions in sports such as the NBA, the NFL, the MLB, or the NCAA.

1. What did Obi-Wan Kenobi mean when he told Luke that Darth Vader was "more machine now than man; twisted and evil"?

MACHINE OR MAN?

2. What does it mean when someone describes another person as "a machine"?

3. Who do you know that could be described as "a machine"?

4. What areas of your life could be described as "a machine"?

5. How might spiritual disciplines, such as Bible study, prayer, church attendance, worship, giving, and serving, turn someone into "a machine of God" rather than "a man or woman of God"?

6. Check out God's strategy to show humans the best way to reconnect with God in John 1:1, 14, 18. Was it more Machine or Man? Why? What was God trying to communicate with all of humanity?

7. What do you think it means to be "human" in our relationship with God, rather than being like "a machine"?

8. Where do you need to give yourself some room to be human in your relationship with God today?

9. Where do you need to become more disciplined in your relationship with God—but without becoming like a machine?

From *Still More High School TalkSheets: 50 Creative Discussions for Your Youth Group* by Dr. David W. Rogers. Permission to reproduce this page granted only for use in buyer's youth group. Copyright © 2009 by Youth Specialties. www.youthspecialties.com

THIS WEEK

Too often we get into a mechanical rut in our approach to a relationship with God. Although spiritual disciplines are good and necessary for growth, God desires for his followers to be human, rather than machine-like.

OPENER

Ask your students to name as many Star Wars characters as they can. Then show scene 15 from *Star Wars Episode VI—Return of the Jedi* in which Luke Skywalker (played by Mark Hamill) is talking with the ghost of Obi-Wan Kenobi (played by Alec Guinness) just after Yoda passed away. Obi-Wan says Darth Vader has become "more machine now than man; twisted and evil." This is the key phrase that will generate the discussion for the TalkSheet. After the clip finishes, take a look at question one.

THE DISCUSSION, BY NUMBERS

1. Darth Vader has lost all sense of what it means to be human because of his thirst for power and his quest to rule with the Dark Side of the Force.
2. When people lose focus on what it truly means to be alive, they can become more "machine" than human, focusing on their goals at the expense of everything and everyone else.
3. Ask for general answers first, such as athletes, doctors, and others who are driven in their professions. Then ask them to name someone they know personally. If appropriate, ask if any family members are like machines in the way they work or respond to the family.
4. Now turn the focus onto your students. Remind them of what Jesus said about noticing the speck in someone else's eye while having a log in your own eye (Matthew 7:2-4). In what areas are they more machine-like? Maybe it's schoolwork, athletics, video games, or relationships.
5. Turn their thoughts toward what it means to have a relationship with God. Explain how these spiritual disciplines, when done with consistency and fervor, can help us grow as followers of Jesus. However, when taken to the extreme, spiritual disciplines can cause people to become so machine-like that they'll mentally "check a box" after they've prayed or gone to church, yet miss the meaning and value of their actions.

6. Have your group read John 1:1,14,18. Of all the ways God could have come to earth, he chose the form of a person. Basically, God wanted to connect with his creation and show them an attainable way back to himself (through Jesus). Let your students wrestle with these challenging concepts. Resist the urge to summarize the discussion for them.
7. Let them know there aren't any wrong answers for this one. It might help to compare their relationship with God to a dating relationship. To be human in a relationship is to have real feelings, faults, emotions, and a continual desire to grow together as they walk through life and learn more about each other. To be like a machine in a relationship is to go through the motions, never express many emotions, and do things out of duty rather than a desire to know the other person.
8. We all need a bit of grace to be human in our relationships with God. Let the group share areas of their lives in which they're not perfect but should allow themselves a bit of room to grow. (Note: This isn't an excuse to sin and stop following after Jesus with your whole life. Rather, it's a chance to acknowledge areas of needed growth without feeling guilty for not being perfect.)
9. Have your group share an area or two in which they need to become more disciplined. You might want to go first to set the tone.

THE CLOSE

Challenge your group to incorporate one thing into their lives this week with a human and heartfelt passion that will enhance their relationship with God. It may be something they referred to in question nine. Have your group share that one thing or one step before closing your time and praying for your students.

MORE

• Have a *Star Wars* marathon party. At different points during the movies, stop to discuss any spiritual themes that arise, such as "good versus evil" and "the Force versus the Holy Spirit." Or compare and contrast the disciples with Jedi apprentices.
• Have your group list as many characters from the Star Wars movies as they can and then match them to comparable biblical characters, based on their roles in the stories and what they stand for or against.

1. Describe a time in your life when all eyes were on you. How did it make you feel?

ALL EYES ON YOU

2. What would be your biggest dream-come-true moment when all eyes would be on you?

3. What would be your biggest nightmare-come-true moment when all eyes would be on you?

4. Read John 13:1-17 and describe why this was an "all eyes on you" moment that we should talk about today.

5. What's significant about what the Father bestowed upon Jesus in verse 3 and what Jesus took off in verse 4?

6. In verse 12 Jesus puts something on and returns to his place at the table. Why do you think these were significant details as all eyes were still on Jesus?

7. What leadership lesson was Jesus trying to convey to his disciples about how they should respond to the people they lead? (See verses 14-15 for a hint.)

8. Who do you know who's in the spotlight quite a bit but chooses to live a servant-leadership lifestyle like Jesus?

From *Still More High School TalkSheets: 50 Creative Discussions for Your Youth Group* by Dr. David W. Rogers. Permission to reproduce this page granted only for use in buyer's youth group. Copyright © 2009 by Youth Specialties. *www.youthspecialties.com*

THIS WEEK

This TalkSheet will examine a time when all eyes were on Jesus. Even though he was the most powerful person in the upper room, he humbly served his friends in a way that spoke volumes to them. Living with humble integrity is an example worth imitating.

OPENER

Start with a quick round or two of flashlight tag. It's simply hide-and-seek in the dark, and the person who's "it" tries to find and tag the other players by beaming them with a flashlight (more details can be found at *www.gameskidsplay.net/games/chasing_games/tag/tag_flashlight.htm*). After the game, debrief with your students. Focus on what it's like when the spotlight hits you. Because it's dark, everyone's eyes focus on whatever is inside the beam of light. Talk about how people experience different emotions in the spotlight. Then share about a time when all eyes were on you. This could be an embarrassing moment, a moment of seriousness, or even a moment of honor and joy. Have the group move on to the TalkSheet and begin thinking about their own spotlight moments.

THE DISCUSSION, BY NUMBERS

1. Let your group share about a time when "all eyes were on them" and how they felt in that moment. This could be a good situation or an embarrassing one.
2. Now have your group share their answers to questions two and three together. Encourage them to dream a bit. Let everyone answer both questions before moving on to the next person.
3. See question two.
4. Let your group describe the "all eyes on you" moment in John 13:1-17. Jesus was getting ready to share the Passover meal with his friends in the upper room when he removed his outer garment and washed his friends' feet. This was a humble demonstration that was normally performed by the servants.
5. Verse 3 indicates that Jesus' heavenly Father had given him all authority and power on earth. Jesus was the most important person there. Jesus knew it, and all the people in the room knew it, too. Verse 4 shows Jesus taking off his outer garment and

wrapping a towel around his waist as he assumed the position of a servant and washed the disciples' feet. Jesus willingly shed his outer symbols of authority (his outer garments) and took the role of a common servant doing the most humble of tasks.

6. In verse 12 Jesus put on his outer clothes before returning to his seat as the host—the most important place at the table. His actions of washing feet, coupled with a return to his place of authority while wearing his symbol of authority (his outer garments), demonstrated to his followers that true leaders don't lord their power over the people they lead. Rather, they lead as humble servants in love and compassion.
7. Jesus didn't just *tell* his disciples how to lead. He took the time to demonstrate how with humility. Jesus didn't ask his followers to do anything or go anywhere that he wasn't willing to do or go himself.
8. Wrap up the discussion by asking your group to identify some people in their lives who demonstrate this type of leadership. How do they act and what is it about their lives that your students admire?

THE CLOSE

Give your group some time to write a letter of appreciation to the person they named in question eight. Provide paper, pens, and envelopes so they can write their letters and mail them this week.

MORE

- **Organize a time for your group to play a big game of flashlight tag—outside and after dark.**
- **Start by showing some examples of embarrassing moments. Google "embarrassing moments videos" and find some clips that would be appropriate to show your group. These will get them laughing and thinking about times in their own lives when they've been embarrassed.**
- **Give your group two video cameras and take them to a public place to stage some crazy stunts that will cause other people to stop and watch. Have one camera record the action and the other record the reactions of the bystanders. One idea is to have someone walk through a busy food court with her arms full of packages. Suddenly she trips, drops everything, gets up, and then falls down again. Challenge your group to get creative with their ideas for things they could do (legally) to cause "all eyes to be on them." After they've captured some good footage, watch it as a group.**

1. It's been said that, "Everyone who wins at anything writes down goals." Do you agree or disagree?

WRITE IT DOWN

2. What are the benefits of writing down your goals?

3. What are the drawbacks of writing down your goals?

4. What are three goals you'd like to accomplish this year?

5. Based on what Jesus says in Luke 14:25-33, what's his view on goals?

6. What makes the least amount of sense to you in this passage?

7. What makes the most sense to you from this passage?

8. What's the primary thing Jesus is trying to convey in this passage?

9. When it comes to being a disciple of Jesus, what are your goals for the next year?

From *Still More High School TalkSheets: 50 Creative Discussions for Your Youth Group* by Dr. David W. Rogers. Permission to reproduce this page granted only for use in buyer's youth group. Copyright © 2009 by Youth Specialties. www.youthspecialties.com

THIS WEEK

The TalkSheet encourages your group to consider the importance of setting goals and counting the cost of achieving them before getting started. Setting goals is one way to know if you're becoming the person you want to be. If you aim at nothing, you'll hit it every time.

OPENER

If you have access to someone in your community who's been on a winning team or achieved goals in athletics or other areas, it would be great if you could invite that person to share her story with the group. The purpose of the testimony would be to convey the importance of not only setting goals, but also counting the cost of achieving those goals. After the person shares her testimony with your students, thank her and move on to the TalkSheet questions with your group.

THE DISCUSSION, BY NUMBERS

1. Have your students consider whether they agree or disagree with the quote and share their reasons.
2. Ask your group to discuss the benefits of setting goals.
3. Then ask your group to discuss any drawbacks to setting goals.
4. Now ask your students to write down three goals they'd like to accomplish—either as individuals or as part of a team—in the coming year. Have them share their goals with the group. Then ask if they've considered the potential costs of achieving these goals. Ask those who answered yes to raise their hand if they're still willing to pursue achieving their goals in spite of the potential costs. (This question will set them up for the passage in Luke 14.)
5. Now have someone read Luke 14:25-33 out loud. Ask the group to offer their opinions about what Jesus thought about setting goals. Hopefully they'll agree that Jesus saw the benefits of counting the costs of a project.
6. This passage has some ideas that may sound a bit strange, such as hating your family in order to follow Jesus (vv. 25-26). Rather than ignore difficult teachings in the Bible, encourage your group to ask questions. Ask them to talk through any parts of the passage that don't make sense. If they mention the verses about hating family, let them know that Jesus wasn't literally advocating hatred toward

family. He was simply making a point that following him requires absolute devotion no matter what.

7. Now ask what made the most sense in the passage. Hopefully they'll discuss the importance of considering the cost of undertaking a project or pursuing a goal. If they don't bring this up, ask them if Jesus' words made sense.
8. Ask them to reread the passage before naming Jesus' main point. Although there are various insights in this teaching, the primary focus is about considering the cost of being a follower of Jesus. Once this is before them, ask why they believe Jesus would talk about considering the cost of being his disciple. Hopefully they'll begin to understand that following Jesus requires dying to oneself. This could explain why Jesus followed the difficult concept of carrying one's cross (verse 27) with a teaching on counting the cost.
9. Now ask them to consider their own relationship with Jesus. Have them think about where they want their relationship with him to be in a year. What do they want to be different about their lives with God? How do they expect to get to the desired places in their relationships? What will they have to do to achieve their goals?

THE CLOSE

Challenge your group to consider the goals they want to achieve in the following areas: Schoolwork, friendships, family, and personal achievements. Ask them to write down their goals during the coming week and share them with the group next time. End the session by praying for your group.

MORE

• **Place an archery target at the front of the room and talk about the importance of having a target. A target is a way to measure how effective one's shooting is. In a sense the bull's-eye could be used to illustrate the goal in the discussion.**
• **Have your students set some group goals for living out their faith over the coming year. These could include goals for attendance, serving others, sharing their faith, and completing a special ministry project together.**
• **Designate four times throughout the year when your group will return to the subject of goals for a "quarterly goal inspection." During these check-in times, they should ask each other about their progress and the price they've paid to succeed.**

ECHOES IN ETERNITY

1. What's the greatest echo that could possibly come forth from a person's life?

2. What's the worst echo that could possibly come forth from a person's life?

3. If the volume level determines the impact of an echo, on a scale of 1 to 10 (with 10 being the loudest), how loud would you say your life is?

4. What would be your echo if your life ended today?

5. What would be your biggest regret if today was your last day on earth?

6. If you knew your life would end next week, what would you do to impact the echo of your life?

7. If you knew you'd live until age 75, what five things would you do to positively affect your echo into eternity?

8. Check out Revelation 4:1-11. Of all the things that could be said throughout eternity, what did the four living creatures in verse 8 say? Write it below. Why do you think they chose to say these words forever?

9. How would your life change if you began living your life with eternity and heaven always at the forefront of your mind and decisions?

From *Still More High School TalkSheets: 50 Creative Discussions for Your Youth Group* by Dr. David W. Rogers. Permission to reproduce this page granted only for use in buyer's youth group. Copyright © 2009 by Youth Specialties. *www.youthspecialties.com*

THIS WEEK

Our lives are meant to have ramifications throughout eternity. This TalkSheet will explore what echoes your group desires to send throughout eternity based on how they choose to live on earth.

OPENER

The opening scene from the movie *Gladiator* shows Maximus (played by Russell Crowe) rallying his troops for battle. He says, "Brothers, what we do in life…echoes in eternity." Show the clip of Maximus' speech to introduce the topic of how our lives echo into and throughout eternity. (Make sure the content of the scene is appropriate before showing it to your group.) After the clip ends, have your students take a look at the TalkSheet.

THE DISCUSSION, BY NUMBERS

1. Ask your group to answer questions one and two before sharing both responses with the group. Make sure they understand that their answers don't have to be about their lives. Rather, it's an echo out of *any* person's life.

2. See question one.

3. For this question, let them rate the volume of their lives on a scale of 1 to 10, with 10 being the loudest. There's no right or wrong answer. Ask them to share why they chose that number.

4. The way your students answer this question may reveal what they think of themselves. Be a good listener and let them share from their hearts. Encourage them to be honest.

5. Have them talk about the biggest regret that would echo into eternity if today were the last day of their lives.

6. Now have them answer as if they know their lives will end next week. What would they choose to do during the next seven days to impact the echo of their lives into eternity?

7. What five things would they like to have echo into eternity if they knew they'd live to be age 75?

8. Have your group read Revelation 4:1-11 and write what the living creatures (particularly in verse 8) are saying that will echo throughout eternity. Ask why they think these beings chose "Holy, holy, holy is the Lord God Almighty, who was, and is, and is to come" as their echo for eternity. What would cause someone to simply echo words of praise and affirmation of who Jesus is throughout eternity? There's no right or wrong answer for this one.

9. Wrap up your discussion by having your group talk about how their lives would be different if they lived every moment with heaven and eternity in the forefront of their minds. What would their decision-making process be like if they trained themselves to do this?

CLOSE

Invite the oldest Jesus-follower you know to close your session by praying over the group. Before the closing prayer, share why you asked this person to pray for your students. Older people often have a greater perspective of eternity and the things in life that truly matter and create worthwhile echoes. Ask the person to pray that these students would live lives that are focused on eternity and would make a difference both in this life and in the life to come.

MORE

• After question eight, have your group repeat the sentence "Holy, holy, holy is the Lord God Almighty, who was, and is, and is to come," for a solid minute—just to get a glimpse of what it would be like to have that echo for the first minute into eternity.

• Watch *Gladiator* together and then discuss the TalkSheet in a cave or a room with great echoes. (Get permission first.)

• Have your students create a list of 10 great things they could commit to doing as a group in the coming year—things that would echo throughout eternity in a meaningful way.

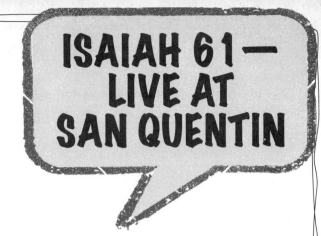

ISAIAH 61—
LIVE AT
SAN QUENTIN

1. Why do you think Johnny Cash chose to do a concert and record a live album from inside a prison?

2. Why did his songs and stories connect so well with the prisoners?

3. In Matthew 25:36, Jesus talks about how visiting prisoners is an action that blesses the heart of God. Do you think Johnny Cash's visit with the prisoners at San Quentin was what Jesus had in mind?

4. Which song do you think the prisoners connected with the most that day?

5. What's one lesson you can learn from Johnny Cash about connecting with people?

6. Read Isaiah 61:1-3. In what ways do you think Johnny Cash did the following:
   • Proclaimed good news to the poor:

   • Bound up the brokenhearted:

   • Proclaimed freedom for the captives and release from darkness for the prisoners:

   • Comforted all who mourn:

   • Provided for those who grieve:

   • Bestowed on them beauty, joy, and praise:

7. Reread Isaiah 61:1-3. In what ways do you think God might want you to—
   • Proclaim good news to the poor:

   • Bind up the brokenhearted:

   • Proclaim freedom for the captives and release from darkness for the prisoners:

   • Comfort all who mourn:

   • Provide for those who grieve:

   • Bestow on them beauty, joy, and praise:

8. If you were asked to coordinate a concert inside a prison, who would you ask to perform?

From *Still More High School TalkSheets: 50 Creative Discussions for Your Youth Group* by Dr. David W. Rogers. Permission to reproduce this page granted only for use in buyer's youth group. Copyright © 2009 by Youth Specialties. *www.youthspecialties.com*

THIS WEEK
This TalkSheet compares the songs from Johnny Cash's *At San Quentin* album with what the prophet Isaiah wrote in Isaiah 61.

OPENER
Before you do anything, read aloud Isaiah 61:1-3. Tell your group that you want them to consider how the life of Johnny Cash could serve as a great example of these words from the Old Testament prophet. Then show the opening scene from *Walk the Line* where Johnny Cash (played by Joaquin Phoenix) is playing a concert inside the Folsom Prison. Afterward, tell your group that Johnny was a big believer in speaking hope and comfort into the lives of prisoners. Then let them listen to the live recording of a concert he performed for the inmates of the San Quentin Prison. The CD is called *At San Quentin*. (Some of the language on the CD may not be appropriate for all audiences, so use good judgment before encouraging your group to listen to the entire CD. You may want to edit the CD into a format that's most suitable for your group.)

THE DISCUSSION, BY NUMBERS
1. After listening to some selections from the *At San Quentin* CD, ask your group to discuss why Johnny Cash chose to record a live album from inside a prison.
2. By listening to the crowd's reactions on the CD, it's clear that the prisoners deeply connected with the music. Have your group discuss why these men connected with Johnny so well.
3. Have someone read Matthew 25:36. In this verse Jesus explicitly makes reference to visiting those who are in prison. Ask your group whether Johnny Cash's visit with these inmates blessed Jesus' heart or if it wasn't quite what Jesus had in mind.
4. List the names of the songs for the group. Although the prisoners seem to enjoy many of the songs on the album, it sounds like they connected the most with the song Johnny wrote especially for them, called "San Quentin." This was the only song they requested he sing again. Perhaps it connected with them so well because the men felt as though Johnny was speaking directly into their lives and situation.
5. Have your group discuss what caused the in-

mates to connect with Johnny Cash. What can your group learn from his life when it comes to connecting with others?
6. Have your group read Isaiah 61:1-3 and give their answers to the following questions based on what they heard on the CD. How do they think Johnny Cash did the following that day?
   - Proclaimed good news to the poor
   - Bound up the brokenhearted
   - Proclaimed freedom to the captives and release from darkness for the prisoners
   - Comforted all who mourn
   - Provided for those who grieve
   - Bestowed on them beauty, joy, and praise
7. Now shift the focus to how God wants your students to do these things for the people in their lives.
   - Proclaim good news to the poor
   - Bind up the brokenhearted
   - Proclaim freedom to the captives and release from darkness for the prisoners
   - Comfort all who mourn
   - Provide for those who grieve
   - Bestow on them beauty, joy, and praise
8. Wrap up the conversation by having each student identify one person or group they'd ask to give a concert from inside a prison. Challenge them to think about who might perform in such a way that would communicate the message of Isaiah 61:1-3.

THE CLOSE
Close your time by having your group write letters to prisoners. Challenge them to write words that will offer the kind of hope found in Isaiah 61:1-3. Encourage them to consider telling the inmates about the group's discussion based on Johnny Cash's *At San Quentin* album.

MORE
• Challenge your group to become involved in a local prison ministry or a reputable national ministry to prisoners, such as Bill Glass Champions for Life.
• Commit to serve prisoners through a project such as Angel Tree, a ministry of Prison Fellowship that serves the children of inmates during the Christmas season and all year round.
• Challenge your group to come up with a "best of" playlist that depicts the message found in Isaiah 61:1-3.

1. List your top five love songs.

LOVE ME DO

2. List your top five movies about love.

3. What's the most creative way to tell someone, "I love you"?

4. What action best demonstrates "I love you" to another person?

5. Read John 14:15, 21. What does Jesus say those who love him will do?

6. What are some of the commands Jesus is talking about?

7. Why might Jesus believe that doing these things (see question five) conveys your love for him?

8. What are other things you do (or could do) that you know God would love?

9. What are things that you do (or could do) that you know your parents would love?

10. How might you creatively love God by loving others this week?

From *Still More High School TalkSheets: 50 Creative Discussions for Your Youth Group* by Dr. David W. Rogers. Permission to reproduce this page granted only for use in buyer's youth group. Copyright © 2009 by Youth Specialties. www.youthspecialties.com

THIS WEEK

This discussion will help your group see that when it comes to loving Jesus, what we do communicates more than what we say. Explore not only what it means to love Jesus by what we do, but also how what we do can creatively and intentionally communicate love to others.

OPENER

Start with a lively rendition of "Love Song Karaoke," where your students can take turns belting out their favorite love songs. You can even make this a competition and vote for the best singer. Have a good laugh and then move on to the first question on the TalkSheet.

THE DISCUSSION, BY NUMBERS

1. Each person should list their top five love songs and then share their lists with the group.
2. Now ask your students to list their top five movies with a "love" theme and share their lists with the group.
3. In his book *The Three Hardest Words in the World to Get Right*, Leonard Sweet suggests that the words *I love you* are sometimes difficult to communicate in ways that are meaningful and genuine to another person. Have your group come up with the most creative ways they can think of to say, "I love you," to someone.
4. Now have your group come up with the one action that best demonstrates "I love you" to another person.
5. Shift the love discussion to a place in the Bible where Jesus talks about what it means to love him. Have them read John 14:15, 21 and write what Jesus says is the proof that people love him. (That people keep his commands.) Ask them to explain why Jesus would say something like this.
6. Have your group write down the commands Jesus is referring to. (Any laws in the Old Testament or that Jesus spoke of in the Gospels will work.) If your students need a little help getting started, point them to the Ten Commandments in Exodus 20. Then have them talk about the things they remember Jesus saying and teaching his followers.
7. Ask your group to take another look at John 14:15, 21 and their answers for question five.

How does keeping Jesus' commands show him love? Let them come up with their own thoughts and then move on to the next question.
8. Your students should now spend a few minutes brainstorming other ways they could demonstrate love that God would love, too. Offer some examples, such as volunteering to do some extra studying with a friend who's behind in a class, even though you don't need the extra study time in that subject. Putting others first blesses the heart of God (Philippians 2:3-4).
9. One thing that makes God smile and shows our love for Jesus is when we keep his command of honoring our parents. (See Exodus 20:12 and Ephesians 6:1-3.) Have your group get creative in thinking of ways to demonstrate love to their parents.
10. Have your group come up with one creative way they'll commit to showing their love for God through a loving action this week. Have them share their ideas and then commit to actually do it.

THE CLOSE

Close by having your group write the names of three people they'll intentionally seek to demonstrate their love to this week. After they have their three names written down, close the session in prayer and ask God to give each student a clear opportunity to demonstrate "I love you" in this way.

MORE
• **Challenge your group to a love song contest. Divide your students into teams and have them come up with the most creative and original love song or piece of poetry. Have each group sing or read their original work for the rest of the group and then determine a winner.**
• **Create an "I love you" art gallery. Over the next month, have students submit different pieces of art that say, "I love you." It can be something they write, draw, paint, compose, videotape, or photograph. Just get them to do something creative and with artistic expression.**
• **Have everyone in the group download the Beatles song "Love Me Do" as a ringtone on their cell phones. Each time their phones ring this week, they'll be reminded to live what Jesus taught in John 14:15, 21.**

1. List your top two greatest movie endings.

2. List your top two worst movie endings.

3. What makes a story ending great?

4. What makes a story ending awful?

5. What scenes would you want included in a movie about your life?

6. What scenes would you want left on the cutting room floor?

7. Read Matthew 25:14-21 and check out how Jesus describes the ending scene from one man's story. What was said and done to the man (see verse 21)?

8. Why did this man have that particular scene as part of his story?

9. Imagine that Jesus asks you to write a script for a movie about your life—from this moment forward. The only thing you have to work with is the ending, when Jesus says to you: "Well done, good and faithful servant!...Come and share your master's happiness!" What other scenes in the movie would lead to that conclusion? How would knowing that ending change the way you approach your life?

START AT THE END

From *Still More High School TalkSheets: 50 Creative Discussions for Your Youth Group* by Dr. David W. Rogers. Permission to reproduce this page granted only for use in buyer's youth group. Copyright © 2009 by Youth Specialties. www.youthspecialties.com

27. START AT THE END—How would knowing the last scene of your life affect all the choices leading up to it? *(Matthew 25:14-21)*

THIS WEEK

How would your students live if they knew the last scene of their lives—if they began each day with this final scene at the forefront of their minds? When we live with the end in mind, life becomes more focused as we make each moment count for eternity.

OPENER

Begin by showing your favorite final scene in a movie. Afterward, tell your group why that scene is your favorite of all the movies you've ever watched. Then tell them they'll be talking about what life would be like if we lived with the final scene of our lives in the forefront of our minds. But first, have them answer questions one and two on their TalkSheets.

THE DISCUSSION, BY NUMBERS

1. Have students share their top two favorite movie endings.
2. Have students share their top two worst movie endings.
3. Give them a few moments to jot down their answers to questions three and four before having them share their thoughts on what makes a great ending to a story.
4. Ask them to share what makes an awful ending to a story.
5. Your group should now talk about the scenes they'd want included in the final cut of the movie about their lives. Remind them that the movie is only two hours long, so some things will have to be edited out.
6. Have them talk about scenes from their lives that they *don't* want to make it into the final cut of their movie. Ask them to consider painful or embarrassing scenes. Encourage your group to be vulnerable during this part of the discussion. Remind them that everybody has these kinds of scenes in their lives. Start with some of your own to set the tone.
7. Now have your group read Matthew 25:14-21 and check out a scene in which Jesus talks about the ending of one man's story. Ask your students to summarize the ending scene (verse 21). (The Master tells the man he's been faithful with the few things that were entrusted to him and since he's

done such a good job, he can enter into his Master's happiness and enjoy his reward.)
8. Have your group talk about why this was the ending that Jesus shared concerning this man's story. Let them wrestle with the question while resisting the urge to share your thoughts.
9. Wrap up the discussion with this final question. How would their script look if they had to start the movie from this point in their lives and the film *must* begin with the final scene. (Jesus tells each person at the judgment seat, "Well done, good and faithful servant!…Come and share in your master's happiness!") How would this future reality affect every other scene leading up to it? Let them share their thoughts before closing the discussion.

THE CLOSE

It's been said that life is lived with meaning and consequence when we "live with the end in sight." It's also been said that we live with conviction and purpose when we "make all of our choices in light of eternity." Have your group jot down LIVE WITH THE END IN SIGHT and MAKE ALL OF YOUR CHOICES IN LIGHT OF ETERNITY. Then challenge them to post these sayings someplace where they'll see them each day. Close your group time by praying that everyone will live with the "Well done…" ending at the forefront of their minds this week.

MORE

• Download the David Wilcox song "Start With the Ending." Then have your students listen to it and discuss its meaning. You may want to print the lyrics and pass out copies of them so your students can refer to the words during the song and throughout the week.
• Have your students check out the first and last chapters of Ecclesiastes. This is a book that starts with the ending ("Meaningless! Meaningless!…Everything is meaningless") and ends right back where it started (Ecclesiastes 12:8). Challenge your group to read this book during the week. It's all about the cycles of life and what really matters when a person tests all the avenues of pleasure, only to find that everything is meaningless except loving God and living for him.
• Create a video montage of great final scenes from movies and show it at the beginning of your time together. Some great possibilities include *Hoosiers, Rocky II, The Natural, Star Wars,* and *Miracle.*

1. Which actor is the master at playing roles filled with awkward moments?

AWKWARD MOMENTS

2. What's the most awkward scene you can think of in a movie or television show?

3. The most awkward moment I've ever experienced in my life was when…

4. Read Luke 9:46-48. What was the awkward moment in this section of the Bible?

5. How do you suppose the disciples felt when Jesus started speaking about what they'd been arguing about?

6. Why did Jesus use a child to help illustrate his point with the disciples?

7. What would be the most awkward moment in the conversation if you and Jesus were to talk about everything going on in your life? Which of your thoughts would he talk about that would make the moment simply awkward?

8. What do you think Jesus would appreciate you doing this week that would also help you take a step toward greatness in his eyes?

From *Still More High School TalkSheets: 50 Creative Discussions for Your Youth Group* by Dr. David W. Rogers. Permission to reproduce this page granted only for use in buyer's youth group. Copyright © 2009 by Youth Specialties. *www.youthspecialties.com*

THIS WEEK

This discussion centers on an awkward moment among Jesus' disciples when they were arguing about which one of them was the greatest. This TalkSheet will help your group think about how an awkward moment might be used to lead your students to true greatness.

OPENER

Have your group watch a scene from season one of *The Office* in which the boss, Michael Scott (played by Steve Carell), must lead the staff through some corporate-mandated diversity training. (Preview the scenes to make sure they're appropriate for your group.) But of course he puts his own spin on the training. Afterward, have your students discuss the most awkward moments in the scene. They should answer questions one and two before moving on in the discussion.

THE DISCUSSION, BY NUMBERS

1. After *The Office* discussion, have your group write the name of an actor who's mastered the awkward moment on either television or in the movies. Have them answer question two before sharing both answers with the group.

2. Have your group select the most awkward scene they can think of (from either television or the movies), in which the actor named in question one has been involved.

3. After they've thought of some fictional awkward moments, have them share about an awkward moment they've experienced. What happened and what did they do?

4. Now shift their focus to an awkward moment in the Bible. Have them read Luke 9:46-48 and discuss what they believe was the awkward moment. The awkwardness came about because the disciples were discussing which of them was the greatest. Then Jesus walked in on their discussion and, knowing their thoughts, launched a true moment of awkwardness. Let your group see if they can come up with something similar in their discussion of the scene.

5. Help them think about what the disciples might have been feeling in this moment when Jesus basically told them what they'd been thinking and talking about in a way that kind of made them feel…awkward.

6. Let them wrestle with this question a bit and don't feel like you have to give them an answer.

7. Now shift the discussion and have your group members focus on their life stories. What would be the most awkward moment for them if Jesus were to start talking with them about their lives? What thoughts would he talk to them about that might make the discussion a bit awkward? Encourage your group to be vulnerable and honest.

8. Remind them of what Jesus said to his disciples at the end of Luke 9:48, "Whoever is least among you all is the greatest." Ask what they can do this week—based upon Jesus' understanding of "greatness"—to help them take a step toward that very thing in their own lives. Have them take a few minutes to share these action steps with the group.

THE CLOSE

Get the cell phone numbers or email addresses of all the students in your group before you dismiss them. Tell them you're going to contact them during the week with a text or email containing these three words: LEAST OR GREATEST? Ask them to choose one of the words to text or email back to you, depending on which one they feel they've been (according to Jesus' definition). This is simply a way to help them stay accountable and remember what was discussed in the group.

MORE

• **Have a TV marathon with your group watching *The Office*. Each time an awkward moment occurs, have your group note it by calling out "AWKWARD!" Count up how many awkward moments there are in each scene and figure out the average awkwardness for each episode.**

• **Divide your group into teams of three and have them come up with their own awkward-moment scenes. (Warning: Set the ground rules ahead of time or this could get out of hand and cross the line pretty quickly!)**

• **If you want to show an example of an awkward moment from a film, then couple *The Office* clip (mentioned above) with a clip from a movie like *Meet the Parents*. In it, Ben Stiller plays Gaylord "Guy" Focker, a male nurse who meets the parents of his girlfriend, Pam (played by Teri Polo), for the first time. (Make sure you preview whichever clip you choose before showing it to your group.) The scene in which Guy is taking a lie detector test for his future father-in-law (played by Robert De Niro) is pretty awkward!**

1. Name some superstitions or sayings that are supposed to bring bad luck.

2. Name some superstitions or sayings that are supposed to bring good luck.

CROSS MY HEART—I'M NOT SUPERSTITIOUS

3. What do you think are the meanings behind these elements of "crossing yourself"?

   • Holding three fingers together (thumb, forefinger, and middle finger) as you make the sign symbolizes…

   • Holding the other two fingers against your palm symbolizes…

   • Dropping the hand from forehead to waist to begin the crossing symbolizes…

   • The upward movement from the waist to the chest symbolizes…

   The final movement from shoulder to shoulder symbolizes one thing if you cross from left to right (left cross) and another if you cross from right to left (right cross).

   • The left-to-right movement symbolizes…

   • The right-to-left movement symbolizes…

4. Read the following passages and explain how each one might have impacted the early Christians in making the sign of the cross.

   • Genesis 4:15

   • Ezekiel 9:3-4

   • Revelation 14:1

   • Revelation 22:4

5. What other outward expressions are used in worship and prayer to help people connect their hearts with God's heart?

From *Still More High School TalkSheets: 50 Creative Discussions for Your Youth Group* by Dr. David W. Rogers. Permission to reproduce this page granted only for use in buyer's youth group. Copyright © 2009 by Youth Specialties. *www.youthspecialties.com*

THIS WEEK

This TalkSheet focuses on the significance of the ancient practice of "crossing" yourself as an act of worship and identifying yourself as a follower of Jesus. Although some may view this simple gesture as a meaningless ritual or empty superstition, its history is filled with sacred and symbolic meaning.

OPENER

Start by asking if they've ever said, "Cross my heart and hope to die; stick a needle in my eye." Make the point that as children—and even adults—we incorporate all kinds of sayings and superstitions that are supposed to bring us either good luck or bad luck. Then have your students answer the first two discussion questions on their Talk-Sheets.

THE DISCUSSION, BY NUMBERS

1. Some examples of bad-luck superstitions and sayings might be crossing the path of a black cat or saying, "Don't step on a crack, or you'll break your mother's back." Let your group share their answers to question one before moving on to question two.

2. Some examples of good-luck superstitions might be rubbing a rabbit's foot or finding a four-leaf clover. If no one brings up "crossing oneself," mention that many people do this whenever they need something good to happen in sports, on a test, or during a difficult time in their life. Then make the point that although some may view this gesture as nothing more than a good-luck superstition, it's actually an act of worship and identification that followers of Jesus have used since the earliest days of the church. Before your group answers question three, share these quotes:

   In all our travels and movements, in all our coming in and going out, in putting on our shoes, at the bath, at the table, in lighting our candles, in lying down, in sitting down, whatever employment occupies us, we mark our foreheads with the sign of the cross.
   —Tertullian, Christian author in the second and third centuries

   Never leave home without making the sign of the cross.
   — John Chrysostom, preacher and theologian in the fourth century

   You should not just trace the cross with your finger, but you should do it in faith.
   — John Chrysostom

3. Now have your group consider the symbolism of the gesture.
   - Holding three fingers together symbolizes the Trinity (Father, Son, and Holy Spirit).
   - Holding the other two fingers against your palm symbolizes the two natures of Christ—human and divine.
   - Dropping the hand from forehead to waist symbolizes Christ's descent to earth.
   - The upward movement from the waist to the chest symbolizes Christ's resurrection.
   - The left-to-right crossing (preferred in Western churches) symbolizes the transition from death to life.
   - The right-to-left crossing (preferred in Eastern churches) symbolizes how Christ descended from the heavens to the earth, and from the Jews (right) he passed to the Gentiles (left).

4. Share how the priests would use a finger or thumb to make the sign of the cross on a person's forehead. This sign was likely in the shape of the Hebrew letter T or the Greek letter X, which represented the names of God and Christ, respectively. Then have them read the following passages and discuss how these Scriptures might have influenced this practice: Genesis 4:15, Ezekiel 9:3-4, Revelation 14:1, and Revelation 22:4. (They all mention markings on the people's foreheads.)

5. Ask your students to talk about other outward expressions or gestures they've either done or seen others do during worship and prayer. Some examples might be kneeling, closing their eyes, folding or raising their hands, clapping, standing in reverence, lying prostrate in submission, or bowing their heads.

THE CLOSE

Have your group pray together and conclude the prayer by crossing themselves as an act of worship and identification as a follower of Jesus.

MORE

- **Have your group search for Psalms that identify outward expressions of worship and prayer.**
- **For the coming week, challenge your students to cross themselves at the start of every day, at the start of each class and extracurricular, before every meal, and at the end of every day. Ask them to share about their experiences with this symbolic gesture during the next meeting.**
- **Give each person a small cross to keep with them as a constant reminder that they're choosing to live as someone who's under the Lordship and guidance of Jesus.**

Based upon the article entitled "Divine Gestures: Why Do Liturgical Christians Make the Sign of the Cross?" by Nathan Bierma as published in Christianity Today, *February 2008, p. 72.*

1. What famous words come to mind when you think about…

   • A president:

   • A world-class athlete:

   • A movie star:

   • A musician:

   • Your parents:

   • Your coach:

   • Your teacher:

   • Your friends:

FAMOUS LAST WORDS—PART 1

2. If you had one chance to say what you really wanted to say before you died, what would be your famous last words?

3. Read Luke 23 and write down Jesus' last words on the cross.

   • v. 34:

   • v. 43:

   • v. 46:

4. If you had to describe each verse with only one word, which words would you choose?

   • v. 34:

   • v. 43:

   • v. 46:

5. Of all the things Jesus could have said, why do you think he chose these as his final words?

6. If you knew you were going to die tomorrow, who would you talk to today to ensure that your last words to them are the ones you want them to remember?

THIS WEEK

This TalkSheet (part one of a two-part series) will focus your group's discussion on what they'd like their "famous last words" and resulting legacy to be. Part one will focus on Jesus' last words on the cross, while part two examines his final words before he ascended into heaven.

OPENER

Start by telling your group that with some people, all we have to do is see an image of their face and we remember famous words they spoke. Show a picture of the following people and see if your students can come up with a famous line that each one said, such as—

- Martin Luther King Jr.: "I have a dream…"
- John F. Kennedy: "Ask not what your country can do for you—ask what you can do for your country."
- Darth Vader (to Luke): "No. I am your father."

Then have your group answer question one on the TalkSheet.

THE DISCUSSION, BY NUMBERS

1. Have your group take a few minutes to come up with a famous phrase or famous words that each person is known for saying. Then have your students share their answers in each category.

2. Ask your group to write down what they'd like their last words to be if they knew they were about to die and had an opportunity to say something memorable. Let your group share their thoughts after a few moments. You may need to set the tone by sharing your own "famous last words."

3. Now shift the focus to what Jesus said as he was dying on the cross. Have them look up Luke 23 and write what Jesus said in the following verses:
   - v. 34: "Father, forgive them, for they do not know what they are doing."
   - v. 43: "Truly I tell you, today you will be with me in paradise."
   - v. 46: "Father, into your hands I commit my spirit."

4. Let your group think about each statement and give their answers, including why they chose each word. Then share your word choice for each verse. The following are just some possibilities.
   - v. 34: Forgiveness
   - v. 43: Hope
   - v. 46: Trust

5. Have your group take another look at the last words of Jesus and give their opinions as to why he chose them. What words might they have said in that situation?

6. Wrap up by asking your group to consider who they'd talk with to ensure that their last words to these people are the best ones. Ask them to list the people they'd want to say something to.

THE CLOSE

Close the session by giving each person a blank piece of paper and a few minutes to write some things they'd want to say to one of the people listed in question six. Remind them that writing a letter allows you to say the things you really want to say exactly the way you want to say them. Challenge your students to deliver their letters this week.

MORE

- **Give your students a blank piece of paper for each person they listed on question six. Then have them write a letter that says the things they want or need to say to each person. Encourage them to deliver their letters in the coming week to make sure they have no regrets.**

- **Create a list of some famous last words—without the names of the people who said them. (Check out *www.corsinet.com/braincandy/dying.html* for some good ones.) Distribute copies of the list to your group and ask your students to guess what's significant about the quotes.**

- **Have your students write the words they want engraved on their tombstones as a remembrance.**

1. **What's the last thing you remember...**

   • Your mom saying to you:

   • Your dad saying to you:

   • Your best friend saying to you:

   • Someone you love who's no longer with you saying to you:

2. **What's the last thing you remember saying to...**

   • Your mom:

   • Your dad:

   • Your best friend:

   • Someone you love who's no longer with you:

3. **Read Acts 1:6-9. What's the last thing Jesus said to his disciples before he ascended into heaven? Why do you think Jesus chose these words as his last?**

4. **Read Luke 24:50-51. What's the last thing Jesus did before he ascended into heaven?**

5. **Of the last words spoken either to you or by you (see questions one and two), how many would you consider to be words of blessing? Write them below.**

6. **Have you ever heard God say something to you? If yes, what was the last thing you heard God say? If no, why do you think you've never heard God say anything to you?**

7. **If you were able to hear God say something to you today, what would you like God to talk with you about? Why?**

8. **What would you prefer God not talk with you about? Why not?**

9. **If God still speaks to people today, in what ways do you think God chooses to speak?**

FAMOUS LAST WORDS—PART 2

From *Still More High School TalkSheets: 50 Creative Discussions for Your Youth Group* by Dr. David W. Rogers. Permission to reproduce this page granted only for use in buyer's youth group. Copyright © 2009 by Youth Specialties. www.youthspecialties.com

THIS WEEK

This TalkSheet is the second part of a two-part series about the last words Jesus spoke (1) on the cross (see part 1), and (2) to his followers before he ascended into heaven. This discussion is about hearing God speak to you. How do we hear God's voice?

OPENER

Start by having your students share their earliest memories. They may be just images or people or perhaps something silly they did as a young child. Let everyone share their earliest childhood memory before turning their attention to the first question on the TalkSheet.

THE DISCUSSION, BY NUMBERS

1. Give each person an opportunity to share the last words they remember hearing from the various people listed. You may need to set the tone by going first.

2. Now flip the focus of the discussion to the last words your students remember saying to each of the people listed. Give your group a couple of minutes to write and then have them talk about their answers.

3. Have your group read Acts 1:6-9 and jot down the situation and the last words Jesus spoke before he ascended into heaven. Jesus told his disciples that although it's not for them to know the time and place about some things, they should know that the purpose God has for them is to be about sharing the Good News of the gospel with people who live nearby, as well as those who live at the ends of the earth. The power of the Holy Spirit will enable them to do this effectively. After your group has come up with something similar, ask them why they think Jesus chose to leave the disciples with this final bit of instruction before he ascended to heaven. Challenge them to think deeply about this question.

4. Now have your group look at another account of this moment. Have your group read Luke 24:50-51 and write the last thing Jesus spoke to his followers. (A blessing)

5. Have your group look back at their answers for questions one and two and discern which statements could be considered a blessing. Have them share the blessings with their group. Now ask the students to label those statements that weren't blessings with another appropriate term (demand, complaint, and so on) and share them with the group.

6. Ask your students if they've ever heard God say something to them. If yes, what was the last thing they heard God say to them? If no, why do they believe they've never heard God say anything to them? Give your group a couple of minutes to think before sharing their responses with the group.

7. Have your group ponder the idea of God talking with them and answer questions seven and eight together. Then ask them to share what they'd like God to speak to them about and why.

8. Now switch the focus and have your group discuss the one thing they *wouldn't* want God to talk with them about and why not.

9. Have your group talk about the different ways that God may speak to them. Some suggestions might be through the Bible, prayer, other people, circumstances, sermons and teachings, nature and creation, dreams, and healthy desires that aren't sinful.

THE CLOSE

Close the time by encouraging each person to complete this simple one-sentence prayer out loud: God, would you speak to me this week about _____? After all have spoken their version of this prayer, wrap up the session by praying over the group and asking God to speak to them before the group meets again.

MORE

• Have your group discuss this quote from Louie Giglio: "The people who hear God's voice the best are the people who know God's Word the most." Translation: God has already said quite a bit to us through the Bible. And God will never say anything that contradicts his words in the Bible.

• Have your group read about a time when God wanted to speak to a young boy named Samuel (1 Samuel 3). What was Samuel's prayer? "Speak, for your servant is listening" (verse 10).

• Challenge your group to pray Samuel's prayer every day this week: "Speak, for your servant is listening." After they do, ask them to sit quietly for five minutes and wait for God to respond to their simple prayer. Have them record anything they sense God telling them and share it with the group the following week.

1. What are the characteristics of someone who's a total success?

TOTAL SUCCESS

2. The definition of a total success is:

3. One thing that symbolizes success is:

4. Based on your answers to the first three questions, name some people who are a total success.

5. Read what Jesus says in Luke 9:23-25. What kind of person is Jesus describing? (see verse 23)

6. What characteristics does Jesus list for a totally successful disciple?

7. How would Jesus define a "total success"?

8. Based on what Jesus said in these verses, what's one thing that would symbolize a total success?

9. Based on Jesus' definition, who's the best example you know of a total success?

10. What's one thing you can do to become more successful (according to how Jesus defines success)?

From *Still More High School TalkSheets: 50 Creative Discussions for Your Youth Group* by Dr. David W. Rogers. Permission to reproduce this page granted only for use in buyer's youth group. Copyright © 2009 by Youth Specialties. *www.youthspecialties.com*

THIS WEEK

This TalkSheet examines what it means to be a total success. Your group probably has some opinions about this. Show them what Jesus has to say and then compare the two definitions. Challenge your group to become the total success that Jesus desires them to be.

OPENER

Start by asking your group to answer this question: **If you could be a total success in any area, what would it be?** Take a few minutes to let your group respond and give their reasons. Then have your group answer the first three questions on their TalkSheets before they share them with the group.

DISCUSSION

1. For these first four questions, let every person answer each question before moving on to the next one. After your group writes the characteristics of a total success, let them share them with the group. Make a master list of the characteristics on a piece of paper or whiteboard for all to see.
2. Ask your students to share their definitions of a total success.
3. Now have your students share one thing that symbolizes success.
4. After they've considered their answers to the first three questions, ask them to create a list of people who they consider to be a total success.
5. Have someone read Luke 9:23-25 and then state whom Jesus is describing in the passage. (Someone who is his disciple.)
6. Make the point that Jesus might describe a total success as someone who is his disciple. Based on this assumption, ask your group to talk about the characteristics of a total success that Jesus mentioned in Luke 9:23-25. Look for answers such as someone who denies himself, someone who takes up his cross, someone who follows Jesus, someone who loses (or gives to others) his life for the cause of Jesus, and someone who isn't worried about gaining the whole world.

7. Have your group come up with a definition of a total success according to what Jesus values. Then have your group share their answers with one another.
8. Ask your group to come up with one thing that would symbolize a total success according to Jesus' definition. Challenge them to think for a bit and then encourage them to share their answers. (It might just be a cross.)
9. Now ask your group to think about people they know (either personally or just know of) and have them write the names of anyone they'd consider to be a total success according to Jesus' description.
10. Ask your students to come up with one thing they could do this week to take a step toward being a total success according to Jesus. It might involve serving someone or taking a stand in a certain situation, even if it's not popular with their friends.

THE CLOSE

Give each person a small cross. Ask them to carry the cross in their pocket this week as a reminder of how Jesus wants them to be a total success. Challenge them to start their day praying with the cross in their hand. Then as they feel the cross in their pocket throughout the day, they should whisper a prayer that God would make them a total success in the way they lay down their lives and serve others—like Jesus calls them to do.

MORE
• **Talk through some ways people might "deny themselves" (Luke 9:23).**
• **Challenge your group to make a list of things they could deny in their lives this week to help them be more like Jesus.**

1. What's the best thing about being a kid?

2. What's the worst thing about being a kid?

3. What's your best childhood memory?

4. What's your worst childhood memory?

5. If you could go back and live one year of your childhood over again, what year would it be and why?

6. If you could go back and erase one year of your childhood, what year would it be and why?

7. A song that many kids learned in Sunday school is "Jesus Loves the Little Children." What do you think Jesus loves about little children?

8. What do the following Bible passages have to say about kids and Jesus?

   • Matthew 7:9-11

   • Matthew 9:23-25, 17:14-18

   • Matthew 11:25

   • Matthew 18:1-4

   • Matthew 18:5-6

   • Matthew 19:13-15

   • Matthew 21:15

9. Finish this statement: To be a kid is to…

From *Still More High School TalkSheets: 50 Creative Discussions for Your Youth Group* by Dr. David W. Rogers. Permission to reproduce this page granted only for use in buyer's youth group. Copyright © 2009 by Youth Specialties. *www.youthspecialties.com*

THIS WEEK

The TalkSheet will focus on Jesus' views on children and their place in his kingdom. By looking back at their own childhoods, your students will have an opportunity to see what Jesus was talking about when he spoke with great love for little kids.

OPENER

Ahead of time, ask your students to bring a baby picture. Display the pictures on a bulletin board and see if they can guess who is who. Make it a competition and give a prize to the person with the most correct guesses. If you aren't able to do this, then bring some of your own baby pictures to share. Talk about the physical traits that still resemble you today before moving on to the TalkSheet questions.

THE DISCUSSION, BY NUMBERS

1. Have your group take a minute to consider what they liked best about being a kid. Ask them to complete this sentence when sharing their answer: "The thing I liked best about being a kid was…"
2. Now have them consider the worst thing about being a kid. Ask them to complete this sentence: "The thing I liked least about being a kid was…"
3. Take the discussion down memory lane and have them share their best childhood memories. You may want to share yours first to get things going.
4. Now flip the question and have them share their worst childhood memories. Be aware that some students may have some pretty painful memories. If appropriate, stop and pray for these individuals.
5. Shift the focus a bit and remind your group that God uses both the good and the not-so-good moments to shape us. Have them choose which year of their lives they'd live all over again if they could. Ask them to share why they'd want to relive that particular year.
6. Now have your students choose which year they'd like to erase from their lives. After everyone has shared, remind the group that even though we may wish a difficult season of life hadn't happened, those can be times when God changes us for the better.
7. Reminisce about their days in Sunday school or Vacation Bible School, learning songs like "Jesus Loves the Little Children." Ask the students to sing or say the words with you now. Then ask your group to discuss what they think Jesus loves about little kids.
8. You can approach this question in a couple of ways: Farm out the passages and have each student (or a smaller group of students) report their findings to the rest of the group. Or have your students look up every passage and write their thoughts before sharing them as part of a group discussion.
   - Matthew 7:9-11 = God gives good gifts to his kids.
   - Matthew 9:23-25, 17:14-18 = Jesus heals kids.
   - Matthew 11:25 = God reveals things about the kingdom to kids.
   - Matthew 18:1-4 = Jesus thinks kids are the greatest.
   - Matthew 18:5-6 = Jesus values kids as precious treasures.
   - Matthew 19:13-15 = Jesus prays for kids and loves them.
   - Matthew 21:15 = Jesus gave kids reason to shout praises to him in the temple.
9. To wrap up the time, go from person to person in the group and have each student complete this sentence out loud: "To be a kid is to…"

THE CLOSE

As your students leave, hand each an index card with these words printed on it:

> Truly I tell you, unless you change and become like little children, you will never enter the kingdom of heaven. —Jesus (Matthew 18:3)

> What needs to change in you to become more like a child this week?

Ask them to text or email their answer to you before they go to bed tonight.

MORE

- Invite a children's choir or Sunday school class to sing songs about Jesus loving children, such as "Jesus Loves the Little Children," "He's Got the Whole World in His Hands," or "Jesus Loves Me."
- Ask some of the parents of your students to write their answers to question three. Then after your group shares their answers to that question, read what the parents wrote about their favorite memories of their kids. If it's appropriate, invite a few parents to the group to share their thoughts and memories.
- As a group, consider sponsoring a needy child through World Vision or Compassion International. This could be a tangible way for your students to love other children and bless the heart of God.

1. Describe an event with the most "spirit" you've ever witnessed.

2. What schools are best known for their "spirit"?

3. Who do you know that lives with "spirit" all the time?

4. Read the following passages from Luke and note how Jesus lived in the power of the Holy Spirit.

   • Luke 1–2

   • Luke 3:16

   • Luke 3:21-22

   • Luke 4:1-2

   • Luke 4:14

   • Luke 4:18 (Isaiah 61:1)

   • Luke 10:21

   • Luke 11:13

   • Luke 12:11-12

   • Acts 1

   • Acts 2

5. Who do you know that lives in the power of the Holy Spirit most of the time? What's different about this person's life?

6. How would your life look different if you lived in the power of the Holy Spirit all the time?

7. What needs to happen in your life for you to begin living in the power of the Holy Spirit today?

From *Still More High School TalkSheets: 50 Creative Discussions for Your Youth Group* by Dr. David W. Rogers. Permission to reproduce this page granted only for use in buyer's youth group. Copyright © 2009 by Youth Specialties. *www.youthspecialties.com*

THIS WEEK

The discussion this week centers on the topic of "spirit." Your group will move from talking about school spirit to Jesus' teachings concerning the Holy Spirit. Imagine what it would look like for a group of students to begin living their lives by the power of the Holy Spirit.

OPENER

Start by talking about the cheers at athletic competitions, such as "We've got spirit! Yes, we do! We've got spirit! How 'bout you?" Have your group name (or even demonstrate) as many different cheers as they can think of. Afterward, have your group divide into teams and have a competition to see who can come up with the best new cheer with the most spirit. After the spirit competition ends, have your group turn their attention to the TalkSheet questions.

THE DISCUSSION, BY NUMBERS

1. Stick with the "spirit" theme and have your group describe their experiences at an event where there was an incredible amount of spirit. Maybe it was a concert, a sporting event, or some type of rally.

2. Let your group debate which schools (college or high school) have the most school spirit. Ask them what spirited traditions take place, such as bonfires, pep rallies, or cheers at sporting events.

3. Have your group shift the focus of their discussion from schools to people. Who lives life with the most "spirit"? Let them use their own definition of what it means to live with "spirit."

4. Have your group look up the following passages about how Jesus lived by the power of the Holy Spirit.
   - Luke 1–2 = Jesus is conceived by the Holy Spirit.
   - Luke 3:16 = Jesus baptizes people with the Holy Spirit.
   - Luke 3:21-22 = The Holy Spirit descends upon Jesus during his baptism.
   - Luke 4:1-2 = Jesus is full of the Holy Spirit and led by the Holy Spirit during his time in the wilderness.
   - Luke 4:14 = Jesus comes in the power of the Holy Spirit.
   - Luke 4:18 = Jesus declares that the Spirit of the Lord was upon him.
   - Luke 10:21 = Jesus rejoices in the Holy Spirit.
   - Luke 11:13 = Jesus promises that God will give the Holy Spirit to those who ask.
   - Luke 12:11-12 = Jesus promises that the Holy Spirit will teach us.
   - Acts 1 = Jesus tells his disciples to wait to begin their ministry until the Holy Spirit empowers them.
   - Acts 2 = The Holy Spirit descends upon the early Christians and empowers them.

5. Let your students talk about a person who lives in the power of the Holy Spirit. If necessary, let them share what they think it means to live by the power of the Holy Spirit. Then have them discuss what's different about that person's life.

6. Now have your students share what their lives might look like if they lived in the power of the Holy Spirit all the time.

7. What changes would they need to make if they truly desired to live by the power of the Holy Spirit?

THE CLOSE

Hand out blank index cards and challenge your students to write down one thing they can do this week to start living by the power of the Holy Spirit. Is there something they need to release to God? Is there a sin they need to confess? Ask them to hand their cards to you as they leave. Text them later in the week to see how things are going.

MORE

- Sometimes living in the power of the Holy Spirit starts by becoming more aware of the Spirit's work and presence. Have your group create some type of reminder that will lead them to think about the Holy Spirit more often. It could be a small sticker on the face of their watch or Post-It notes with the initials "H. S." written on them.
- Set up three lamps with light bulbs of varying wattages to illustrate the difference in brightness of a 40-watt bulb, a 60-watt bulb, and a 100-watt bulb. Explain how the wattage increases the brightness of the bulb. Then compare this illustration to lives that are being fully lived by the power of the Holy Spirit with those that are lived in their own power.
- Take a field trip to a local college sporting event and have your group observe what type of "spirit" the crowd has during the game.

1. List three things that put you "on edge."

2. List three things that put you "at ease."

3. List the characteristics of a person who puts you "on edge."

ON EDGE OR AT EASE?

4. List the characteristics of a person who puts you "at ease."

5. From a relational standpoint, identify whether the following people put you "on edge" or "at ease" and why.
   • Parents:

   • Siblings:

   • Teachers/Coaches:

   • Friends:

   • Adults in Authority:

   • Total Strangers:

6. Why might people say that the following puts them "on edge"?
   • Religious People:

   • Jesus:

7. Why might people say that the following puts them "at ease"?
   • Religious People:

   • Jesus:

8. Read Luke 5:27-35. What may have caused people to feel "on edge"?

9. Reread Luke 5:27-35 and write what may have put people "at ease."

From *Still More High School TalkSheets: 50 Creative Discussions for Your Youth Group* by Dr. David W. Rogers. Permission to reproduce this page granted only for use in buyer's youth group. Copyright © 2009 by Youth Specialties. *www.youthspecialties.com*

THIS WEEK

This TalkSheet compares the rigid religious leaders with the unhurried and thought-provoking life of Jesus. The Pharisees, with their superior attitudes and lists of rules, put people "on edge." Jesus, with his compassion and simple yet straightforward truth, put the irreligious "at ease." Which approach will your students take?

OPENER

Hold an "on edge" versus "at ease" taste test. There are various ways to do this. However, the main objective is to get students thinking about and experiencing (via taste) items that might be categorized as either "on edge" or "at ease." Blindfold a few volunteers to be the "testers" and let the rest of the group enjoy watching their responses. Once the contestants are blindfolded, show the crowd each food item and ask for a show of hands as to whether the item will be voted "on edge" or "at ease." Don't let the contestants know how the crowd voted. Then let the blindfolded students taste the food and share their decision. Some "on edge" foods might be lemons, horseradish, onion, jalapeño pepper, salt, steak sauce, and spicy mustard. Some "at ease" foods might be warm chocolate, strawberries, ice cream, cheesecake, and breath mints. After the taste test finishes, move the group's focus to the TalkSheet questions.

THE DISCUSSION, BY NUMBERS

1. Have each person list three things that put them "on edge" and let them share their list with the group.
2. Now have each person list three things that put them "at ease" and let them share this list with the group.
3. Ask your students to consider the characteristics of people who put them "on edge." Let them share their answers and keep a running list on a whiteboard or large piece of paper so your group can process this question together.
4. Now ask them to list characteristics that cause them to feel "at ease" with someone. Let them share their answers with the group after a few minutes of reflection.
5. Have your group identify whether the following list of people puts them "on edge" or "at ease" and why. They may wish to answer "Both" on some of these choices. If so, just have them share their reasons.
   - Parents
   - Siblings
   - Teachers/Coaches
   - Friends
   - Adults in Authority
   - Total Strangers
6. The point of this question is to get your group talking about their perceptions regarding the stereotypical "religious person" who puts people "on edge" as compared to the way Jesus might put people "on edge." Let your group write their thoughts about each and then share them with the group.
7. Now have them share their thoughts about how both "religious people" and Jesus might put people "at ease" with the things they say or do.
8. Have your group read Luke 5:27-35. Jesus is having a dinner party with some new friends, and the Pharisees and teachers of the law are putting people "on edge" by complaining about the company Jesus keeps. They also question Jesus as to why his disciples don't fast and pray. However, Jesus and the disciples weren't bothered by their criticisms. They go on eating and drinking and enjoying themselves.
9. Have them reread the passage and find examples of Jesus putting others "at ease." Jesus befriends a tax collector who didn't have many friends. He called the tax collector by name and invited him to go with him. Later, Jesus attends a big party at his new friend's house, along with other tax collectors and sinners. Instead of throwing a bunch of religious talk at them, Jesus eats and drinks and enjoys the party. Jesus tells insightful and meaningful stories that cause people to think. He also pursues relationships with all kinds of people.

THE CLOSE

Wrap up your time by asking your group to talk about whether they tend to put others "on edge" or "at ease."

MORE

- **Have your students make two lists: (1) Things they do that cause people to be "on edge," and (2) things they do that cause people to be "at ease."**
- **Ask your students' parents to make a list of the things their children do that put them or others "on edge" or "at ease," just to offer your students another perspective.**
- **Have your group write down one thing they can do this week to put someone else "at ease." Then have them write down one thing they can eliminate from their life that causes someone to feel "on edge" when they're around.**

1. Next year I expect to…

2. I have high expectations when it comes to…

3. I have low expectations when it comes to…

4. I never expected _____,
   but it's a reality.

5. When it comes to relationships, what's expected
   from you and what do you expect from your—

	They Expect…	I Expect…
• Parents		
• Siblings		
• Friends		
• Teachers		

6. What do people expect from Jesus?

7. In what ways did the expectations and realities match (or not match) in the following passages concerning Jesus?
   • Matthew 1:18-25 (Jesus' earthly father)

   • Mark 10:17-31 (rich young ruler):

   • Luke 23:32-39 (He saved others. Why won't he save himself?)

   • John 3:1-21 (How can a man be born again?)

8. Why do you think God sometimes responds with actions that don't match our expectations? Has this ever happened in your life?

9. The question has been raised: "Is God disappointing you, or do you have the wrong expectations of God?" Where might this be true in your life?

GREAT EXPECTATIONS

From *Still More High School TalkSheets: 50 Creative Discussions for Your Youth Group* by Dr. David W. Rogers. Permission to reproduce this page granted only for use in buyer's youth group. Copyright © 2009 by Youth Specialties. www.youthspecialties.com

THIS WEEK

This TalkSheet will help your group consider the expectations people have in various relationships and how they respond to them. What do you expect from others? What do others expect from you? What do you expect from God? If we're disappointed with God, then maybe we have the wrong expectations.

OPENER

Ask your group, by a show of hands, how many of them expect to get married. Then ask them to create a list of expectations for their future spouses and a list of things their spouses should expect from them. If you have a coed group, let the guys work together on a list of expectations for wives and the girls make a list of expectations for husbands. Then compare their lists. Segue to the TalkSheet by making the point that at every stage of life, we'll have expectations about things and people, just as people will have expectations about us.

THE DISCUSSION, BY NUMBERS

1. Have your group answer questions one through four before the group discusses them. After they finish the sentences, go back to question one and let each person share their answers to all four questions before allowing the next person to share.
2. See question one.
3. See question one.
4. See question one.
5. For each relationship, they should write down the expectations people have of them, as well as their expectations for these people. Discuss each category as a group.
6. Now talk about people's expectations of Jesus. Make this a two-part question, focusing on what people expect of Jesus today and then what people expected of Jesus when he walked the earth.
7. Divide your students into four teams and give each group a passage to study before sharing their findings with everyone.
   - Joseph (Matthew 1:18-25) = Joseph wasn't expecting to be the father of someone else's child. Joseph planned to quietly divorce Mary. However, God changed Joseph's expectations through a dream. Joseph learned that this son would one day save the people from their sins. This wasn't what he expected his son to do.
   - Rich young ruler (Mark 10:17-31) = This wealthy man expected Jesus to give him some rules to follow or to encourage him to keep doing what he'd been doing to inherit eternal life. Giving all of his wealth to the poor and following Jesus wasn't the answer he expected to hear.
   - Nicodemus (John 3:1-21) = This man was seeking something from Jesus that isn't spelled out here. However, Nicodemus decided he wanted what Jesus offered him instead. As he and Jesus continued talking, Nicodemus didn't understand the expectations for seeing the kingdom of God.
   - People at the cross (Luke 23:32-39) = Jesus' followers and the religious experts both expected Jesus to save himself. They expected that the true Messiah would do such a miraculous act. Even one of the criminals hanging next to Jesus expected this.
8. There doesn't have to be a definitive answer to this question. Allow your group to wrestle with the difficulty of why our expectations of God don't always match up with God's reality in our lives. Ask your group to share a personal example, if possible.
9. This is the heart of the matter when it comes to our expectations and the way we respond to reality. It's a weighty concept that might need to be considered, rather than immediately digested and regurgitated in the form of a thoughtful response.

THE CLOSE

Read Isaiah 55:8-9—"For my thoughts are not your thoughts, neither are your ways my ways," declares the LORD. "As the heavens are higher than the earth, so are my ways higher than your ways and my thoughts than your thoughts." Understanding an infinite God from a finite perspective sometimes leads to unmet expectations. When this happens, encourage them to take a step back and ask God to give them his perspective.

MORE

• **Invite students to share about how they once had great expectations for their lives, but their expectations were never met. Instead, God had a different set of expectations, and their lives took a different course.**
• **Have a pregnant woman (a first-time mother) share her expectations of what motherhood will be like.**
• **Have an engaged couple share what they expect marriage to be like. Then have a couple who's been married for 50 years share what their marriage has been like versus what they expected it to be.**

1. What's one thing you can "do in your sleep"—you don't even have to think about it?

HALF- OR WHOLEHEARTED?

2. What's one thing you can do but only if you really think about what you're doing?

3. In what areas of your life are you just going through the motions?

4. Read 2 Chronicles 25:1-2 and write what it says about King Amaziah in verse 2.

5. Is this a good characteristic or a bad characteristic? Why?

6. What happens when you do the right thing but without the right heart?

7. What do you do in life that's right, but your heart isn't into it?

8. What would happen if your heart was fully involved in (passionate about) whatever you wrote for question seven?

9. What do you wish you could do with wholehearted devotion?

From *Still More High School TalkSheets: 50 Creative Discussions for Your Youth Group* by Dr. David W. Rogers. Permission to reproduce this page granted only for use in buyer's youth group. Copyright © 2009 by Youth Specialties. www.youthspecialties.com

40. HALF- OR WHOLEHEARTED?—Living well before God with wholehearted devotion and emotion (2 Chronicles 25:1-2)

THIS WEEK

This week's discussion is about living a life that honors God and doing so with wholehearted devotion. So often we simply "go through the motions" and our hearts aren't into the things we do. What would happen if we became more intentional and passionate about our approach to life?

OPENER

Start by making the point that there are some things we do that require very little attention or thought. In a sense we can "do them in our sleep." To prove your point, ask your students to get out their cell phones and text the following message to you: I CAN DO THIS IN MY SLEEP. The only catch is that they must do it with their eyes closed. Give a prize to the first person who texts you—with no mistakes. After you've had a little fun with this opener, direct their attention to the Talk-Sheet questions and have them answer question one.

THE DISCUSSION, BY NUMBERS

1. Have your group talk about one thing they don't even have to think about when they do it. Get them thinking about the stuff they do without any thought or emotion or intentional "heart" behind it.

2. Now have them share one thing they can do only if they give it their undivided attention. Thus, if they don't focus, there's no way they can do it.

3. Make the point that there are some areas of our lives in which we're just going through the motions and our minds and hearts aren't fully engaged. Ask your group to talk about one such area of their lives.

4. Ask them to read 2 Chronicles 25:1-2 and write down verse 2: "He did what was right in the eyes of the LORD, but not wholeheartedly."

5. Ask them to answer questions five and six together and then discuss their conclusions with the group. Challenge them to give examples to support their reasoning. Remember, part of the learning process means allowing them to wrestle with the hard questions of their faith. Don't feel like you have to have this one resolved before moving on to question seven.

6. See question five.

7. Move from a philosophical discussion to a more personal one. Have your students share one thing they do that's "right to do" but their hearts aren't into it. An example might be obeying their parents on an issue like curfew or chores.

8. Now challenge them to think about what might happen if they chose to put their hearts and minds into this half-hearted action. At the very least, how would it affect their relationships with God, let alone the other people involved?

9. Shift directions for this last question and have them dream a bit with you. Ask them to consider one thing they wish they could do with wholehearted devotion. This could be an opportunity they don't currently have. It could also be something they're doing now, but only half-heartedly, and they wish God would change their hearts.

THE CLOSE

Give each student a paper heart and instructions to write down a word or phrase to represent an area in their life that's lacking wholehearted devotion. Challenge them to take the heart everywhere they go this week to remind them of the discussion. Encourage them to take a few minutes throughout the day to pray about this issue as they ask God to change them from being half-hearted to wholehearted.

MORE

• **Incorporate a couple of other "in your sleep" contests to open up the time together. Some options might be tying one's shoes, putting on a coat and buttoning it up, making a peanut butter and jelly sandwich—all with their eyes closed.**

• **Have your group take a look at what Jesus says in Revelation 3:15-16 about half-heartedness versus wholeheartedness, but using temperatures to describe the situation. How might these words enlighten the conversation?**

• **Consider showing your students Provident Films' "Wholehearted" video, which uses a football practice scenario to powerfully illustrate the point of how we need to live our lives wholeheartedly (available at www. sermonspice.com/videos/2488/wholehearted/).**

1. What questions about your life would reveal the following Magic 8 Ball answers?

- As I see it, yes:

- Ask again later:

- Better not tell you now:

- Cannot predict now:

- Concentrate and ask again:

- Don't count on it:

- It is certain:

- It is decidedly so:

- Most likely:

- My reply is no:

- My sources say no:

- Outlook good:

- Outlook not so good:

- Reply hazy, try again:

- Signs point to yes:

- Very doubtful:

- Without a doubt:

- Yes:

- Yes—definitely:

- You may rely on it:

WHAT DO YOU KNOW?

2. If you could ask God three questions about your life and he would answer you, what three questions would you ask?

3. Read 1 John 4:11-17 and write down what these verses say we know.
- What does verse 11 say we can know about God?

- What should be our response?

- How does verse 12 say God lives in us and God's love is also made complete?

- What can we know in verse 13?

- What did the Father send the Son to do in verse 14?

- How do we know God lives in us according to verse 15?

- What are we to know and rely on according to verse 16?

- How is love made complete according to verse 17?

4. Who do you know that needs to know this truth in their own life?

From *Still More High School TalkSheets: 50 Creative Discussions for Your Youth Group* by Dr. David W. Rogers. Permission to reproduce this page granted only for use in buyer's youth group. Copyright © 2009 by Youth Specialties. www.youthspecialties.com

THIS WEEK

This TalkSheet uses the example of a child's toy to illustrate the things we wish we could know versus the things the Bible tells us we already know regarding God's love.

OPENER

Bring a Magic 8 Ball to the session. You're going to have some fun with a hypothetical situation, but first make it very clear to your students that God does not speak to people through a Magic 8 Ball. Now, just for kicks, ask your students to consider these questions: *What if God chose to communicate with us through the Magic 8 Ball? What would you want to know?* Have your group ask some yes-or-no questions, which you then ask the Magic 8 Ball, and reveal the answers. Some questions might be:

- Will "so-and-so" pass his test this week?
- Does "so-and-so" have a chance at getting her curfew extended?

Again, this is simply to get your group thinking about things we want to know versus the things God has already told us we know (because the Bible tells us so). After some time, have your group take a look at the TalkSheet.

THE DISCUSSION, BY NUMBERS

1. For this first question, explain that they should approach it as though they're contestants on *Jeopardy*. Twenty Magic 8 Ball responses are provided, so they just need to come up a question about their lives that would best match each answer. For example, "As I see it, yes" might be linked to "Should my parents increase my allowance?" Give your group a few minutes to come up with their questions, and then let them share what they wrote.

2. Now that you've had some fun, make sure they understand that God doesn't communicate through a Magic 8 Ball. However, remind them that God does tell us some specific things that we can know about our lives. Ask to write down three questions for which they'd love to know the "for sure" answer straight from God. Ask them to share what they wrote.

3. Point out that sometimes God allows us to know the answers to our questions sooner rather than later, but not usually. One thing we can know for sure, however, is what God says to us through the Bible.

Have your group read 1 John 4:11-17 and respond to the questions listed.

- What does verse 11 say we can know about God? (God loves us.)
- What should our response be? (We should love others.)
- How does verse 12 say God lives in us and God's love is also made complete? (If we love one another.)
- What can we know in verse 13? (He has given us his Spirit, thus allowing us to know that we live in him and he in us.)
- What did the Father send the Son to do in verse 14? (To be the Savior of the world.)
- How do we know God lives in us according to verse 15? (If anyone acknowledges that Jesus is the Son of God.)
- What are we to know and rely on according to verse 16? (The love God has for us.)
- How is love made complete according to verse 17? (In this world we are like Jesus.)

4. God allows us to know things not only for our own benefit, but also for the benefit of others. Ask your group to think about people who need to know about God's love. Have them write a name and then move on to The Close. Use your best judgment when considering whether to allow your students to share that person's name or initials with the group.

THE CLOSE

Take a few minutes to allow your group to pray for the person they listed in the last question. Encourage them to ask God for opportunities to share with this person what the Bible says we can "know." Wrap up by praying that God would give each student the courage to share these things they "know" with others this week.

MORE

- **Have each student write down one yes-or-no question at the very start of the session. Put their questions in a bowl and let the Magic 8 Ball answer them. For fun, have the group try to determine who submitted each question.**
- **Organize a night to shoot pool with your group. Play games of eight-ball in which the goal is to shoot the black eight ball last. Then, at some designated time between games, take a break to work through the TalkSheet.**

1. Read Psalm 15. What does it mean to be a person who…
- v. 2 Has a walk that is blameless

- v. 2 Does what is righteous

- v. 2 Speaks the truth from his heart

- v. 3 Has no slander on her tongue

- v. 3 Does his neighbors no wrong

- v. 3 Casts no slur on others

- v. 4 Despises those whose ways are vile

- v. 4 Honors whoever fears God

- v. 4 Keeps her oaths even when it hurts

- v. 5 Lends money to the poor without interest

- v. 5 Doesn't accept bribes against the innocent

FIRST-DAY SCHOOL SUPPLIES

2. Which characteristic is most evident in your life?

3. Which characteristic needs the most work in your life?

4. Write the name of someone who demonstrates each characteristic on the list below. Select a different name for each characteristic.
- Has a walk that is blameless
- Does what is righteous
- Speaks the truth from his heart
- Has no slander on her tongue
- Does his neighbors no wrong
- Casts no slur on others
- Despises those whose ways are vile
- Honors whoever fears God
- Keeps her oaths even when it hurts
- Lends money to the poor without interest
- Doesn't accept bribes against the innocent

5. What do verses 1 and 5 say are the benefits of having the characteristics mentioned in this Psalm?

From *Still More High School TalkSheets: 50 Creative Discussions for Your Youth Group* by Dr. David W. Rogers. Permission to reproduce this page granted only for use in buyer's youth group. Copyright © 2009 by Youth Specialties. www.youthspecialties.com

THIS WEEK

This TalkSheet will walk your students through Psalm 15 so they can examine the list of characteristics that are needed for someone to dwell in God's sanctuary.

OPENER

One thing many young kids enjoy is having new school supplies for the first day of class. Have your group make a list of items that probably appeared on their supply list in elementary school, such as crayons, No. 2 pencils, erasers, glue, scissors, notebook paper, and folders. Now turn their attention to Psalm 15, which contains another list that people who desire to dwell in God's sanctuary must be aware of. Read Psalm 15:1-5 out loud to your group. But before you begin, ask them to count the listed traits of a person who can dwell in God's sanctuary. After reading the Psalm, ask your group how many characteristics they heard. (Answer: 11.) Now have your group turn their attention to the TalkSheet.

THE DISCUSSION, BY NUMBERS

1. Have your students write down what each of the characteristics from Psalm 15 means. Encourage them to write definitions, scenarios, and personal examples that will help your group apply these characteristics to real life. What does it mean to be a person who…
   - v. 2 Has a walk that is blameless
   - v. 2 Does what is righteous
   - v. 2 Speaks the truth from his heart
   - v. 3 Has no slander on her tongue
   - v. 3 Does his neighbors no wrong
   - v. 3 Casts no slur on others
   - v. 4 Despises those whose ways are vile
   - v. 4 Honors whoever fears God
   - v. 4 Keeps her oaths even when it hurts
   - v. 5 Lends money to the poor without interest
   - v. 5 Doesn't accept bribes against the innocent

2. Ask your group to review the list from Psalm 15 and choose the one that's most evident in their lives right now. Have them share the reasoning behind their choice and perhaps a personal example to support it.

3. Now have them select one characteristic from Psalm 15 that they believe needs the most work in their lives. Again, have them share a reason why

they selected that characteristic and a personal example, if possible.

4. Have your group write a different name for each of the characteristics listed in question one. Who do they know that exhibits each of the characteristics and what examples can they share to support their answers?
   - Has a walk that is blameless
   - Does what is righteous
   - Speaks the truth from his heart
   - Has no slander on her tongue
   - Does his neighbors no wrong
   - Casts no slur on others
   - Despises those whose ways are vile
   - Honors whoever fears God
   - Keeps her oaths even when it hurts
   - Lends money to the poor without interest
   - Doesn't accept bribes against the innocent

5. Have your group take a look back at verses 1 and 5 in Psalm 15. What are the benefits of being a person who exhibits the characteristics in this Psalm? Verse 1 says such a person may dwell in God's sanctuary and live on his holy mountain. Verse 5 says such a person "will never be shaken." Have your group wrap up the discussion by talking about why such things would be benefits.

THE CLOSE

Ask your group to look back at their answers for questions two and three. Challenge them to write down an action step they can take this week to build on their strength from question two and to improve on their weakness from question three. Close your time by praying for your group.

MORE
- **While you're talking about school supplies, have your group explore how their supply lists changed from elementary school to junior high to high school.**
- **Invite an elementary school teacher to join you in the discussion starter. Ask her to bring her school-supplies list and examples of the supplies her students would bring on the first day of school. This could be especially fun if you invite one of your students' favorite elementary school teachers.**
- **Use this topic to spur a group service project. Work with a local elementary school to organize a school-supplies drive for low-income families. Have your group collect the necessary items that can be given to needy children for their first day of school.**

1. What are the benefits of having vision and being able to see the big picture?

SEEING THE BIG PICTURE

2. What are benefits of not having vision and not being able to see the big picture?

3. Read Proverbs 29:18 and write down what that verse means to your life.

4. In what areas do you feel like you have vision and see the big picture in your life?

5. In what areas do you feel like you lack vision and seem to be drifting in your life?

6. In the next year, what would you like the picture on the puzzle box to look like concerning:

   • Relationship with your parents:

   • Friendships:

   • Academic goals:

   • Life experiences:

   • Family goals:

   • Career goals:

7. What do you think Proverbs 28:19 has to do with question six?

From *Still More High School TalkSheets: 50 Creative Discussions for Your Youth Group* by Dr. David W. Rogers. Permission to reproduce this page granted only for use in buyer's youth group. Copyright © 2009 by Youth Specialties. *www.youthspecialties.com*

THIS WEEK

This discussion will help your group understand the value of seeing the big picture. Having a clear vision of our goals not only helps us focus our plans and efforts to achieve those goals, but also prevents us from merely drifting along in life with little focus and clarity.

OPENER

Divide your students into two groups and see which one can complete a small jigsaw puzzle first. Give both groups the same puzzle; however, only one group gets to have the box. Have the groups work in two different rooms so they don't know that one group doesn't have a picture of the completed puzzle. Simply tell them the puzzles are identical and let them go at it. The first one to finish their puzzle is the winner. (Most likely, it will be the group with the box top.) Bring the groups back together and tell them that one group was able to see "the big picture" and one wasn't. Make the point that when you have a picture of the end goal in mind, it's easier to tell if you're making progress toward that goal. Direct their attention to the TalkSheet.

THE DISCUSSION, BY NUMBERS

1. The point of these questions is to get your group thinking about having vision and seeing the big picture. You may want to refer to the picture on the puzzle box to illustrate the point.

2. Now ask your group to talk about any possible benefits of *not* having vision and *not* having the big picture in mind. Things like being a "free spirit" and "going with the flow" are some possibilities.

3. Give them a moment to offer some thoughts. Then have them write down the King James Version of this same text: "Where there is no vision, the people perish." Ask your group to discuss what this means. After a few moments, share that the Hebrew word for *perish* is *chazon*, which means "to drift." Thus, where there's no big picture or understanding of where you're headed, people begin to drift along without intentional purpose.

4. Let your group discuss the areas of their lives in which they believe they do have vision, such as relationships, priorities, where they'll attend college, what they'll study, and so on.

5. Now flip the question and ask them to discuss the areas of their lives in which they lack vision and are drifting along without intentionality or direction.

6. Show your students the puzzle box and make the point that in order to know how to put the pieces together, it's helpful to have the big picture to refer to. Likewise, in order to move through life in the best way possible, it's helpful to have a vision and clear picture of what we're hoping for and pursuing in life. Challenge your group to think outside the box and list some descriptive words and phrases that create a picture of what they want each of the following areas to look like:
   - Relationship with your parents:
   - Friendships:
   - Academic goals:
   - Life experiences:
   - Family goals:
   - Career goals:

7. Hopefully someone will say something about the importance of having a vision for where they want to go in life to keep them moving forward, rather than just drifting through life and hoping to land at their desired destinations.

THE CLOSE

Challenge your group to write descriptions of what they want the pictures or goals of their lives to look like five years, 10 years, and 20 years from now. Putting the big picture before them will help them avoid drifting through life and ending up in the sea of regret and missed opportunity.

MORE

• Give each person a small picture frame as a reminder that when they have a clear picture of where they're headed, it will help them to stay on course and not drift.

• Before your next meeting, challenge your group to search in magazines and online to find images that symbolize the picture they'd like to put before them in the areas listed in question six. Have them bring their pictures to the next session and process them together. Ask why they chose those pictures and what they represent or symbolize.

• Invite a guidance counselor to share some practical tips that your students should consider when setting life goals for the next five, 10, and 20 years. Perhaps there's a life coach in your congregation or community who'd be willing to share some helpful strategies as well.

1. If you were a contestant on *Who Wants to Be a Millionaire* and needed to use the Phone-a-Friend Lifeline, who would you call and why?

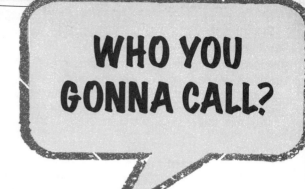

WHO YOU GONNA CALL?

2. Describe a time when you had to make an important or difficult decision and you needed some input from other people.

3. If you could select only five people to ask for advice, who would they be and why?

4. What advice do the following verses offer that you should consider when making decisions for your life?

- Psalm 119:24

- Proverbs 1:5

- Proverbs 3:7

- Proverbs 10:14

- Proverbs 12:15

- Proverbs 13:1

- Proverbs 13:20

5. Which of those seven verses resonated the most with you and why?

6. What's one thing in your life that you need to get wise counsel about before moving forward?

From *Still More High School TalkSheets: 50 Creative Discussions for Your Youth Group* by Dr. David W. Rogers. Permission to reproduce this page granted only for use in buyer's youth group. Copyright © 2009 by Youth Specialties. *www.youthspecialties.com*

THIS WEEK

This discussion revolves around the importance of knowing who's speaking into your life about the decisions you make. The Bible is full of advice about listening to wise people who offer godly counsel. Who will your students call when they need wisdom and advice for their lives?

OPENER

Start by asking for examples of television game shows (past and present) that give contestants the best odds at winning the most money and why. If nobody mentions *Who Wants to be a Millionaire*, be sure and do so. This show offers decent odds because there are three Lifelines that each contestant can use (one time each) to help answer the series of trivia questions—50:50, Ask the Audience, and Phone-a-Friend. Ask the group to look at their TalkSheets and begin thinking about who they'd call if they needed to use Phone-a-Friend.

THE DISCUSSION, BY NUMBERS

1. Have your group talk about which friend they'd call, some reasons why they selected that friend, and how helpful they'd be at answering trivia questions.

2. Ask your group to share about making an important or difficult decision. What was the situation and why did they feel it was necessary to get input from others?

3. Have your students list the top five people they'd choose to ask for advice regarding important life decisions. Why did they choose those five?

4. Divide your students into smaller groups and assign a few verses to each. Then let each smaller group share their findings with everyone to keep the discussion moving.

   • Psalm 119:24—"Your statutes are my delight; they are my counselors." The baseline of all wisdom is God's Word. Taking advice from the Bible will never steer me wrong. Anything that contradicts the Bible isn't counsel I want to follow.

   • Proverbs 1:5—"Let the wise listen and add to their learning, and let the discerning get guidance." Listening will help me learn and understand where to walk in the wise paths.

   • Proverbs 3:7—"Do not be wise in your own eyes; fear the LORD and shun evil." My opinion doesn't matter that much when it comes to wisdom. One wise approach to life is to fear God and move away from all evil.

   • Proverbs 10:14—"The wise store up knowledge, but the mouth of a fool invites ruin." To become wise means to continue seeking wisdom from others. Talking too much isn't a good thing.

   • Proverbs 12:15—"The way of fools seems right to them, but the wise listen to advice." What looks right to someone who isn't wise may actually be foolish. It's a good thing to at least listen to advice, whether or not I take it.

   • Proverbs 13:1—"A wise child heeds a parent's instruction, but a mocker does not respond to rebukes." Mom and Dad have stuff to share that's worth listening to. Talking back or ignoring what they say isn't wise.

   • Proverbs 13:20—"Walk with the wise and become wise, for a companion of fools suffers harm." Surround yourself with wise people and you'll eventually become like the company you keep. The same is true if you surround yourselves with fools.

5. Ask your group to look back over those verses and talk about which one resonated the most with them and why.

6. Now have them consider their present lives. Ask them to name one area or situation for which they need to seek advice from wise people.

THE CLOSE

Give your group some helpful guidelines for choosing the most appropriate sources of advice.

   • Talk to more than one person.

   • Seek out people who will tell you the truth, not just what you want to hear.

   • Seek out people who are farther down the road of life than you are.

   • Before you talk with someone, ask God to speak to you through that person.

   • Before acting on any advice, make sure it's not contrary to God's Word.

Wrap up the discussion by having them write the names of the people they'll approach to get this needed advice (see question six).

MORE

• **Start by playing a few rounds of *Who Wants to Be a Millionaire* to get the competitive juices flowing. (www.millionairetv.com/playonline.html)**

• **Invite some of the students' parents to share how they choose the people from whom they ask advice. Have them name some of the people they consult.**

• **Challenge your group to come up with a list of ways to become a person of wisdom whom others will call when they need advice or input about life.**

1. What's the last promise you made to someone?

2. What's the last promise someone made to you?

3. What's the biggest promise you've ever made?

4. What's the biggest promise someone has ever made to you?

5. What's the biggest promise you've ever broken?

6. What's the biggest promise someone has ever broken to you?

7. What's the most illogical promise you've ever made?

8. What's the hardest promise you've ever had to keep?

9. What promises does God make to his people in the following verses?

   • Romans 8:28

   • 1 Corinthians 10:13

   • Hebrews 13:5

10. Which promise from question nine is the most difficult one for God to keep?

From *Still More High School TalkSheets: 50 Creative Discussions for Your Youth Group* by Dr. David W. Rogers. Permission to reproduce this page granted only for use in buyer's youth group. Copyright © 2009 by Youth Specialties. *www.youthspecialties.com*

THIS WEEK

This TalkSheet will guide your group's discussion about making promises. Each day people make promises to each other—some of which are kept, and some of which are broken. God also makes promises throughout the Bible. God still stands by his promises to this day.

OPENER

Start by having your group talk about the significance of a promise ring. (It would be good to have some type of ring to hold up as an illustration.) After they've discussed this concept, have them talk about the differences in the intentions, as well as the various degrees of promises, between a promise ring, an engagement ring, and a wedding ring. After a few minutes of brainstorming about these three types of rings, direct them to the TalkSheet questions to continue the discussion.

THE DISCUSSION, BY NUMBERS

1. Now that your group is thinking about promises, give them a few minutes to answer the first eight questions on the TalkSheet before discussing them with the group. Allow all of the students to share their responses before moving on to the next question. You want them thinking about different promises they've made and received.
2. See question one.
3. See question one.
4. See question one.
5. See question one.
6. See question one.
7. See question one.
8. See question one.
9. Make the point that although people don't always follow through on their promises, God does. Have them look up the following promises of God and jot down what each one says.
    - Romans 8:28—God promises to take everything that happens in the lives of those who love God and work them together for a good purpose in the end.
    - 1 Corinthians 10:13—God promises not to allow us to be tempted beyond what we can handle, and he'll always provide a way of escape from that temptation so we can endure it.
    - Hebrews 13:5—God promises never to leave you or forsake you.

Take a few minutes to process these promises as a group. Probe your students a bit to see what they really think about them. Do the promises seem illogical or untrue in any way? Encourage them to wrestle with the magnitude of such promises. What do these types of promises say about God and his commitment to his people? Is God offering a promise ring, an engagement ring, or a wedding ring with such promises? Remind your students that God keeps his promise no matter how recent, big, illogical, or difficult it might be. God's promises are like a wedding ring that's placed on the finger of his people. God will never break his promises—vows—to his people. He won't "file for divorce" or walk away from anything he's promised.

10. Ask your group to consider which promise would be the hardest for God to keep and why.

THE CLOSE

As you wrap up this discussion, remind your group that the only person you can control in terms of keeping a promise is *you*. Challenge your group to think about the current stage of their relationship with Jesus: Are they wearing a promise ring, an engagement ring, or a wedding ring? Although the Bible teaches us to be cautious about making vows or promises before God, ask them to write down some "potential promises" they believe God might be leading them to make concerning their relationship with Jesus. In a sense, have them write their "vows to Jesus." What do they want their relationship to look like? Then close your time by praying over your group and asking God to help make these considerations a reality and a commitment in the coming days.

MORE

- **Have your students write a preliminary set of "vows" about being the person God desires them to be—both now and in preparation for their future spouse.**
- **Follow up this TalkSheet with an emphasis on sexual purity and promising to wait until marriage to become sexually active. (Check out *www.lifeway.com/tlw/* for more information about the True Love Waits campaign.)**
- **Encourage your group to count up how many times God promises something to his people in the Bible. Have them email their findings to you or bring them to the next group meeting.**

1. List as many rivals as you can think of.

RIVALS

2. If you had to identify one rival in your life, who or what would it be?

3. If God were to identify a rival, who or what do you think it might be?

4. Read Luke 16:13-15 and write down what Jesus had to say about two rivals.

5. Why do you think Jesus identified these two things as having a rivalry for our loyalties, attention, and affection?

6. Now read Matthew 6:19-21. How does this passage relate to Luke 16:13-15?

7. What might be an effective way to keep money from rivaling God in your life?

From *Still More High School TalkSheets: 50 Creative Discussions for Your Youth Group* by Dr. David W. Rogers. Permission to reproduce this page granted only for use in buyer's youth group. Copyright © 2009 by Youth Specialties. *www.youthspecialties.com*

THIS WEEK

It seems as though wherever there's competition, there are rivals for dominance. As your group processes the concept of rivalries, they'll begin to see that the greatest rival God has for our attention, affection, and loyalty can be our stuff. But Jesus said people cannot serve both God and money.

OPENER

Start by having your group take the Pepsi Challenge. In 1975 the Pepsi-Cola corporation began an advertisement campaign encouraging the public to decide which soda they preferred in a simple taste test: Pepsi or Coca-Cola. Pepsi claims that more people preferred the taste of Pepsi. So let everyone in your group take the taste test and see which one wins.

THE DISCUSSION, BY NUMBERS

1. These rivals can be sports teams, such as the New York Yankees and the Boston Red Sox; food chains, such as McDonald's and Burger King; or even fashion brands, such as Nike and Adidas. The possible categories are endless, so encourage your group to think broadly. After giving them a few minutes to work, take some time and let each person share.

2. Have the students identify an object or person that they'd consider to be their rival. This could be a school, person, challenge, or whatever they think of when they think of their own rival. After they've made their selection, have everyone share what they wrote down and why.

3. Flip the focus to God's main rival. Ask them to consider how God would have answered question three. After they have a few moments to think about it, let them share their ideas and why.

4. Have your group look up Luke 16:13-15 and write down what Jesus says concerning God's main rival. In this passage Jesus is talking about the subject of money and loyalty. In verse 13 Jesus says a person "cannot serve both God and Money." In a sense, Jesus is identifying a person's money, possessions, or stuff as being a chief rival to the loyalty, attention, and affection of God.

5. Ask your group to process why they think Jesus selected money as God's main rival. Give them time

to talk through their answers and reasoning before moving on to the next question.

6. Have them look up Matthew 6:19-21. Point out that one of the best ways for people to understand what God thinks is to allow Scripture to help us interpret Scripture. Thus, by looking at both of these passages, we begin to get a clearer picture of what Jesus is talking about when it comes to the potential for money, possessions, and our stuff being a big rival for God's place in our lives. If your group doesn't mention it, help them see that Jesus is teaching that our hearts and our money (treasures) are somehow linked.

7. Have your group process ideas for ways to make sure their stuff doesn't become a rival for their affection and loyalties toward God. The most effective—yet sometimes the most difficult—way is to give away part of our money and possessions. Being generous toward others helps us view our treasures as belonging to God.

THE CLOSE

Give your students a penny and ask them to read the phrase on the back: IN GOD WE TRUST. Encourage them to take this penny everywhere they go and let it serve as a reminder of the "God versus Money" rivalry. Challenge them to decide which "God" they'll "trust in." Is it Jesus or is it their stuff? Encourage them to either hold the penny or keep it before them to help them focus when they pray.

MORE

• Have your group take a personal inventory of how they spend their money. In Matthew 6:21, Jesus teaches that our money and our hearts are invariably linked. Where does your students' money go? If they have their own checking accounts, have them look at their register to see where they're spending it each month. Most people tend to have a greater interest in the things they spend their money on.

• If some of your students go to rival high schools, have them engage in a friendly challenge the next time their schools compete against each other. For instance, when their football teams meet, have the group agree that students from the losing school must wear the school colors or logo of their rival to the very next meeting. Let your group come up with any additional challenges to make the competition more engaging for the winning and losing teams.

THE GAP

1. List some examples of a gap between what people say they believe and what they actually practice.

2. Who do you know that has the smallest gap between what she believes and what she says and does?

3. What's the big deal about having a gap between what we say we believe and the way we live?

4. Read what James 2:14-17 has to say and paraphrase these verses in your own words.

5. After reading this passage, what examples of the gap come to mind? (They should be different than what was discussed in question one.)

6. Beth Moore wrote, "The gap between our theology and our reality is so wide we've set ourselves up for ridicule." Do you agree or disagree? Explain.

7. One area of my life in which I don't have much of a gap between what I believe and what I live is…

8. One area of my life in which I need to close the gap between what I believe and what I live is…

From *Still More High School TalkSheets: 50 Creative Discussions for Your Youth Group* by Dr. David W. Rogers. Permission to reproduce this page granted only for use in buyer's youth group. Copyright © 2009 by Youth Specialties. *www.youthspecialties.com*

THIS WEEK

This TalkSheet will help your group talk about the importance of closing the gap between what we say we believe and what we live out in our everyday lives. Closing the gap demonstrates to a watching world what it means to follow Jesus.

OPENER

Take a plate of Double Stuf Oreo cookies and make a big deal about how you *believe* this is your favorite cookie. Make sure you use the word *believe* because at the end of the object lesson, you'll make the point that your beliefs and your actions have a gap between them. (In other words, you're a Double Stuf Oreo hypocrite.) Tell your group there are lots of different ways to eat Double Stuf Oreos—

- All in one bite
- Eating the top cookie first, then the white filling, and then the bottom cookie
- Taking off the top cookie, eating the white filling, and then eating both chocolate cookies
- Dunking the cookie in milk

Now demonstrate one way to eat a Double Stuf Oreo that *isn't* acceptable. Take off the top of the cookie, remove the white filling (don't eat it), and then eat the chocolate cookies. The point you're trying to make is that the Double Stuf Oreo isn't really your favorite cookie because you left a major component (the white filling) sitting on the plate. There's a gap between what you say you love and what you really love. What you love is the chocolate cookie. To truly love a Double Stuf Oreo, one has to love both the chocolate cookies and the white filling. In a sense, you've just admitted to being a Double Stuf Oreo hypocrite because there's a gap between what you say you believe and what you practice. Acknowledge that this demonstration is a goofy way to make the point. Now that you have them thinking about the gap, have them move on to the first question on their TalkSheets.

THE DISCUSSION, BY NUMBERS

1. This first question is intended to get them talking about issues of hypocrisy. Let your group talk through some of these different scenarios, and then move the conversation to the next question.
2. Have your group members think about someone who's consistent in what she believes and lives. Let

your students identify a person with the smallest gap between belief and practice, and then have them give examples to support why they selected that person.
3. Ask the group to talk through why they believe it is (or isn't) a big deal to have a gap in our lives. Encourage them to think a bit more about this question and why they think or feel the way they do about the gap.
4. Ask someone to read James 2:14-17 out loud. Then encourage everyone to put the passage into their own words. Let a few students share their paraphrases before moving on to the next question.
5. Mention how you started this conversation by asking your group to list situations that portrayed a gap between what someone believes and what he practices. After reading and paraphrasing James 2:14-17, ask them to write down any new examples that came to mind. After giving them a minute to jot down their answers, let your group share their ideas.
6. Ask your students to consider the quote from author and teacher Beth Moore. Do they agree or disagree? Let your group wrestle with the concept and then move on to the final two questions.
7. Have your group answer questions seven and eight before revealing their answers to the group. Challenge them to really think about this concept of "the gap" in their lives. After they've completed the sentences, let every student share both responses before moving on to the next person.
8. See question seven.

THE CLOSE

Give copies of the Beth Moore quote and James 2:14-17 to your group. Then close your time by praying that God will help your students close the gap between what they believe and what they practice. As you dismiss them, challenge your group to memorize the passage this week.

MORE
- **Enjoy Double Stuf Oreos and milk with your group before dismissing.**
- **Give each student one Double Stuf Oreo to take with them as a tangible reminder to close the gap this week (provided they don't eat it on the way home).**
- **Check out YouTube for some funny videos and songs about Oreos.**

1. List as many examples of fads and timeless items as you can for these 10 subjects.

FAD OR TIMELESS?

	FADS	TIMELESS
• Songs		
• Clothes		
• Sayings		
• Food		
• Movies		
• TV Shows		
• Cars		
• Hairstyles		
• Toys		
• Sports		

2. What criteria did you use to determine whether something should be considered a fad or timeless?

3. What do you think being "relevant" has to do with fads or timelessness?

4. "Things that are eternal are always relevant." How does this concept relate to our discussion of fads and timeless items?

5. Read Hebrews 13:8 and write it below. Do you think it describes a fad or a timeless person? Explain.

6. What difference does that verse make in your life?

From *Still More High School TalkSheets: 50 Creative Discussions for Your Youth Group* by Dr. David W. Rogers. Permission to reproduce this page granted only for use in buyer's youth group. Copyright © 2009 by Youth Specialties. www.youthspecialties.com

THIS WEEK

This TalkSheet allows your group to examine various fads, while comparing them to things that stand the test of time. The discussion will eventually lead your students to look at the timeless One who is the same yesterday, today, and forever and how Jesus' immutability affects their lives.

OPENER

Start by showing or talking about some fads from your past. Make yourself the illustration for today by wearing an outfit and hairstyle that used to be "the style." Remind your students that we all have fads in our past—and possibly our present. However, the things that stand the test of time are called *timeless*. Ask your group to take a look at the first question on their TalkSheets.

THE DISCUSSION, BY NUMBERS

1. Divide your students into small teams of two or three people and give them 10 to 15 minutes to answer both the first and second questions (concerning the criteria they used to determine whether something was a fad or timeless). Ask the teams to share their answers for question two before naming the fads and timeless items they came up with for each of the 10 subjects.

2. See question one.

3. Part of what makes something a fad is the public's perception that it's "relevant" only for a season. Ask your group to consider what relevance has to do with something being tagged as a "fad" or "timeless."

4. Now take the concept of relevance a bit further with your group. Have them consider this statement—"Things that are eternal are always relevant"—before unpacking what it means in terms of whether something is labeled a fad or timeless.

5. Have your students read Hebrews 13:8 and write the verse on their TalkSheets. Then ask them to decide which term—*fad* or *timeless*—best describes what the verse is saying and write that word beside it.

6. Ask your group to talk about what Hebrews 13:8 has to do with their lives. See what they come up with, and then point out that this truth has massive ramifications for their identities. If we base our identities on something that changes with the seasons or with our seasons in life, then it stands to reason that our identities will change just as frequently. Conversely, if we base our identities in One who never changes, then who we are remains consistent, regardless of the changes that take place around us—what we wear, what activities we do, where we go, who we hang out with, or where we go to school. If our identities are grounded in the timeless, eternally relevant, and unchanging nature and character of Jesus, then no matter what season of life we happen to be in, we can stay the same in terms of who we are in Christ and what our life is about as one of his followers.

THE CLOSE

Wrap up by challenging your students to wear an out-of-style outfit to school or church this week as a way to remember that fads come and go. Remind them that Jesus is the same yesterday, today, and forever. Close your time in prayer.

MORE

• **Have a "Fad Party" and encourage your group to wear clothes that were once a fad but are no longer considered "in style." Play music selections that were once "in" but are now "out." Serve "fad-dy" foods from the answers your group came up with for question one.**

• **Enjoy a "Fad Movie Marathon" with your group and watch some of the movies your students named in question one.**

• **Challenge your group to wear the exact same outfit every day for one week. Make it simple, like a plain white T-shirt, jeans, and shoes. That way the same "look" could be worn each day without having to wear the exact same shirt and jeans (or do laundry every night). As people ask, "Didn't you wear that yesterday?" encourage your students to share why they're wearing the same clothes yesterday, today, and tomorrow. It's an easy and natural way to begin a conversation about Hebrews 13:8 and the unchangeable nature of Jesus.**

SPENDING THE NIGHT

1. The last time I spent the night away from home was…

2. The first time I remember spending the night at a friend's house was…

3. The last time I stayed up all night was…

4. The most fun I've ever had spending the night away from home was…

5. The worst memory I have of spending the night away from home is…

6. The greatest thing about spending the night away from home is…

7. The worst thing about spending the night away from home is…

8. If I had to spend the night at somebody's house for a whole month, it would be _____

   because _____.

9. Three things you must do when spending the night away from home are…

10. Three things I'll never do again when I'm spending the night away from home are…

11. Read Luke 6:12. What did Jesus do while spending the night on a mountainside?

12. What's the longest amount of time you've spent praying to God?

13. What do you pray about the most?

14. What's the hardest thing for you when it comes to praying?

15. What's the last thing you prayed about?

16. Describe a time in your life when you know God answered your prayers.

17. Describe a time in your life when God stayed silent in response to your prayers.

18. What's the most pressing thing you need prayer for today?

From *Still More High School TalkSheets: 50 Creative Discussions for Your Youth Group* by Dr. David W. Rogers. Permission to reproduce this page granted only for use in buyer's youth group. Copyright © 2009 by Youth Specialties. *www.youthspecialties.com*

THIS WEEK

Through this TalkSheet your students will consider what happens when they spend the night away from home and then discuss their prayer lives, including the amount of time they spend praying, as well as some things they need to pray about today.

OPENER

Start by sharing a story or two about the friends you liked to spend the night with when you were growing up and the things you used to do at their house. Then have your group take a look at their TalkSheets and answer the first 10 questions.

THE DISCUSSION, BY NUMBERS

1. After everyone has finished answering questions one through 10, let your group share their responses. Get everyone's answers to question one before moving on to question two.
2. See question one.
3. See question one.
4. See question one.
5. See question one.
6. See question one.
7. See question one.
8. See question one.
9. See question one.
10. See question one.
11. Now ask your group to read Luke 6:12 and write down how Jesus spent the night one evening. The verse says, "One of those days Jesus went out to a mountainside to pray, and spent the night praying to God."
12. Before letting your students answer question 12, give them a few moments to consider what it would have been like for Jesus to pray on the side of a mountain all night long. What do they think he was praying about? Why did he do it at night instead of during the day? Why did he pray for so long in one sitting? Then ask them to share the longest amount of time they've ever spent in prayer. Let them share their answers before moving on to the next question.
13. Now ask your group to share about the thing(s) they pray about most consistently.
14. Acknowledge that sometimes it can be difficult to pray for an extended period of time—sometimes it's difficult to pray at all. Ask them to talk about the hardest thing for them when

it comes to spending time in prayer. What are their biggest obstacles when they try to pray? Give them a few moments to think about their answers before letting them share.

15. Ask your group to share about the last thing they remember praying about. Let each person take a turn.
16. Now ask your students to share about a time in their lives when God answered their prayers. You may want to share something from your own life to set the example. Encourage them to give a bit of context to their prayer but keep it brief.
17. Now ask them to share about a time when they felt like God responded to their prayers with silence. Again, feel the freedom to share an example from your own life. When your students are sharing, be careful not to say too much in response. Sometimes it's fine to let people share how they perceive God to be working and how they're feeling about an issue without commenting on everything they say.
18. Ask your group to write down the one thing in their lives for which they feel a pressing need for prayer. Allow your students to share their responses with the group before moving on to The Close.

THE CLOSE

Close your time by asking the students to get into groups of two or three and pray for one another about the issues they mentioned in the final question.

MORE

• Challenge your group to write down their prayers this week as a way to stay focused and be intentional about their communication with God. Then ask them to allow time to sit and see if God has any response for them. Remind them that prayer is a two-way conversation, rather than a one-way lecture.
• Challenge your students to spend one solid hour in prayer sometime this week.
• Invite your entire group to spend one night together (either at someone's home or at the church) and pray for the entire evening. If you don't want to literally spend the night together, you could divide up the night and assign students to pray during certain hours throughout the night. You could focus your night of prayer on an upcoming special event that you want your group to pray about, such as a camp, retreat, or mission trip. Challenge your group to push themselves spiritually in such disciplines as prayer.

1. The greatest Christmas gift I ever wanted and received was…

2. The greatest Christmas gift I never knew I wanted but received was…

3. The best Christmas gift I ever gave to someone else was…

ANYTHING YOU WANT

4. If Christmas were tomorrow, I'd really want to receive…

5. If God offered to give you anything you wanted, what would you ask for and why?

6. Read 2 Chronicles 1:1-17. What did Solomon ask God to give him (verse 10)?

7. Why do you think Solomon wanted these things?

8. Why do you think God was so pleased with Solomon's request?

9. What's one thing you could do this week to become wiser?

From *Still More High School TalkSheets: 50 Creative Discussions for Your Youth Group* by Dr. David W. Rogers. Permission to reproduce this page granted only for use in buyer's youth group. Copyright © 2009 by Youth Specialties. www.youthspecialties.com

WEEK

alkSheet is designed to get your group talk-
bout what they'd request from God if they
w God would give them whatever they want-
. When King Solomon was given this opportunity, he asked God for wisdom and knowledge and
pleased God with his selfless request.

OPENER

Start by showing the scene from *A Christmas Story* in which Ralphie (played by Peter Billingsley) asks Santa Claus for a Red Ryder BB Gun (scene 24 on the DVD, "Slippery Santa Slide"). After the clip, ask your group to look over the TalkSheet and begin thinking about Christmas presents they've received in the past.

THE DISCUSSION, BY NUMBERS

1. Have your group complete the sentences for questions one through four before sharing their answers with the rest of the group. Let every person share their answers for question one before moving on to question two.
2. See question one.
3. See question one.
4. See question one.
5. Now shift the question a bit and have your group think about what they'd want if they knew God would give them whatever they asked for. Ask them to think seriously about this. Let your group share their answers with the rest of the group.
6. Have your group read 2 Chronicles 1:1-17 and write down what King Solomon requested from God in verse 10 (wisdom and knowledge). Make sure your group sees that God initiated the proposition (verse 7).
7. Now ask your group to talk about why Solomon wanted wisdom and knowledge. According to verse 10, he wanted to lead his people well. He obviously understood the magnitude of his responsibility as the king.
8. Continue the conversation by having your students talk about why God was so pleased with Solomon's request. Verse 11 says God was pleased because Solomon's selfless request (he didn't ask for wealth or accolades or the death of his enemies) would benefit so many (God's people who lived under Solomon's reign).
9. Finally, ask your students to consider an action step that would move them toward becoming a wise person. Let them share their answers with the group before wrapping up the discussion.

THE CLOSE

Invite the wisest person in your church to pray over your group and ask God to grant your students wisdom and knowledge. Ahead of time tell your group why you believe this person is the wisest person in the church. Before he prays, ask him to share any tips he might have about how to become a person of wisdom.

MORE

• **Gather your group and watch *A Christmas Story* together before pulling out the TalkSheet and working through the questions.**
• **As a group, provide "Christmas" for a needy family in your community.**
• **Challenge your students to meet regularly with a wise adult. Suggest that your students approach a wise person they know and ask if this person would be open to mentoring them toward greater wisdom.**